HORSE & BAMBOO:

A JOURNEY

FOREWORD

This is a story of a journey. The journey spans forty years between 1978 and 2018 during which time I founded and mostly directed the work of Horse & Bamboo Theatre. This story is about the development of the company's creative work, in particular the touring theatre shows, but also many other productions that were developed during those years.

Horse & Bamboo still exists as a company, although it's very different from the one that came together in 1978. The focus is now on serving a local community. It is still based in Waterfoot, Rossendale, and hosts a range of creative activities and provides a home for other artists and arts groups. It runs arts workshops in prisons, an annual local Wakes Week, and a regular arts programme of events for babies and toddlers, as well as activities including film, music and game nights.

Horse & Bamboo took its name from the company's horse-drawn tours, which occupied the spring and summer months between 1979 and 2000. The company was one of the many radical and experimental UK theatre groups that blossomed between the 1960s and the 1980s. In retrospect these were golden years for British theatre.

CONTENTS

1. The Ballad of Ellen Strange, 1978   7
London – Stevenage – Manchester – Rossendale – the importance of stories

2. Horse-drawn Theatre   15
Welfare State – managing horses

3. Pictures From Brueghel, 1979   21
Teaching – a Bread & Puppet connection – the first tour

4. The Home-made Circus, 1980   29
Matrogoth – administration

5. Little Heads (Shouldn't Wear Big Hats), 1981   33
New premises – my role – Leicester Festival

6. The Woodcarver's Story, 1982   36
Woolmer Green – an early inspiration – the marquee – a pilgrimage

7. The Whitworth Horse, 1982   42
Village life – Walter Lloyd – the Horse Fair and a large fire

8. Guided Imagery, 1981 – 2006   48
Mythic drama – a new challenge – funding issues

9. Needles in a Candleflame, 1983   52
Reorganization – China Men – Joyce Laing

10. Seol, 1984   57
Jenny Wilson – Father Colin – Scots Gaelic – the Outer Hebrides

11. The Manchester Crib, 1984   65
A wooden crib and a dedication performance - music

12. Tales From a Maskshop, 1986   71
Another move - Rawtenstall – using a narrator

13. The Wheel/An Roth, 1987/8   75
Irish Gaelic - injuries – a memorable sea crossing

14. Pilton residency, 1987   79
The Beaford Centre – curlicues

15. Plaited Path, 1989   85
Kantor – a Drama company

16. The Wish, 1990   88
Adventures in Northern Ireland – motorised touring - masks

17. The Flood, 1991   95
I stop touring

18.   A Strange & Unexpected Event, 1992   99
Mexico – JG Posada – Hungary

19.   Westminster Abbey, 1994/96   105
Canon Harvey – problems with Christ – a political storm

20.   Dance of White Darkness, 1994   113
Maya Deren – 'voodoo' – Orkney, and a potential crisis – Hungary and beyond

21.   Visions of Hildegard, 1994-6   119
Rehearsal time – back at the Abbey

22.   The Legend of the Creaking Floorboard, 1997   123
Gog and Magog – touring the Netherlands

23.   Harvest of Ghosts, 1999   127
Dr. Sam Ukala – 'folkism' – casting success – a last word from Sam

24.   The Girl Who Cut Flowers, 2000   135
Alison Duddle arrives from the US

25.   A Period of Change   139
An end to horse-drawn touring – The Boo opens

26.   Company of Angels, 2001-4   142
A breakdown – co-directing with Alison – a US tour

27.   Working with children and young people   145
A show for the Royal Exchange – Alison's new direction – Guo Yue

28.   Stocktake 1   149

29.   Veil, 2008   151
Our Board of Directors – big ambitions – The Lowry – the 'Crash'

30.   Deep Time Cabaret, 2011   156
Limbo – a new approach – performing under ground

31.   Angus - Weaver of Grass, 2012/13   160
Back to the islands – Joanne B. Kaar – a thank you to Creative Scotland

32.   Stocktake 2   167

33.   Different Moons, 2014-18   169
Our local South Asian community - Apna

34.   The Moonwatcher 2018   178

Cast lists   183

Acknowledgements & Credits   185

First published March 2024
www.bobfrith.co.uk

Text copyright ©2024 Bob Frith
Photographs copyright ©2024 Bob Frith (exceptions noted)
Layout David Chatton Barker
Edit support Jill Penny
The right of Bob Frith to be identified as the author of this work has been asserted by him in accordance with the Copyright, Designs & Patents Act 1988. All rights reserved.
ISBN: 978-1-3999-8384-6
A catalogue record for this book is available from the British Library.

Cover photograph: At the Callanish Stones, Lewis
End papers: From Angus, Weaver of Grass, 2012

HORSE & BAMBOO:
A JOURNEY

BOB FRITH

1. THE BALLAD OF ELLEN STRANGE 1978

I was nine. My parents made the decision to move our family away from a London still pitted with ruins left by wartime bombs to a new town in search of the good life. Stevenage was a place that was disconcertingly spotless and clean and things were, mostly, at right angles to one another. After the sitting and passing of my 11-plus exam I spent the next seven years at the local grammar school, a pompous institution which liked to pretend it was a public school. This was generally a flat time for me, but I managed to make some good friends, and the art master allowed us the run of the art room, which made life considerably more bearable. Finally, when the time came to move away, the wheel of fortune brought me to Manchester, an impossibly exotic destination, and to its equally exotic art college.

During my degree years at the college (1967-71) the fashionable approach to painting was to create neat, grid based cool abstractions. These generally reminded me too much of Stevenage. Rather I enjoyed paintings that suggested stories of different kinds, and these inevitably tended towards the figurative. This was frowned on by most of the young and eager art tutors, but I somehow managed to side-step the problems that some of the other students experienced, possibly because I was lucky enough to win a number of prizes and awards during those years.

At the end of the first, exciting and life-changing Foundation year, I discovered Rossendale, sixteen miles north of Manchester, nestled among the foothills of the Pennines. One reason I was drawn to the place was the richness of textures everywhere. There was the moorland, tight little river valleys packed with trees, untidy stone buildings, ginnels, hills to climb, gruff but friendly locals - and the stories.

From the 1970s on I was using those local stories in my work, especially in my printwork. At one stage I was banned from the Helmshore British Legion because an exhibition of prints in Haslingden Library hinted at stories that some of the Legion committee members felt were still too raw, and should have remained untold.

There was one very old story about a young woman named Ellen Strange. Apparently Ellen had been murdered by her lover while they were walking the old moor-top road to Edgeworth. I was told that back in the day locals had erected a memorial cairn at the precise spot where she lost her life. This was on moorland not far from the old terraced cottage in Helmshore that I had rented. So, on the next suitably fine day, I hiked up the hill to take a look.

Just off the moorland track to Edgeworth, a thousand foot up where you might have expected to find only cotton grass and tufts of reed, stones were scattered all around. You wouldn't exactly call it a cairn, but it looked like what might happen to a cairn if it had been forgotten about and left to nature and sheep for a few decades. The location of the stones was where I was told that the cairn should have been, so I took a day out and rebuilt it on the spot where the stones had been most plentiful.

I wanted to make art that people like my neighbours in Helmshore would enjoy. By now I had had a few exhibitions of my work, and the appeal of showing at art galleries was starting to lose its novelty....too polite, too impersonal.

The image of the flattened cairn, rebuilt, restored, resonated strongly with me and it would continue to resonate through those early years of exploration and creation with Horse & Bamboo. In the moment, it seemed like something I could build an event around. So I went to the Local History room at Haslingden Library, and looked through their collection of old books. Here I came across the 'Ballad of Ellen Strange', written early in the nineteenth century by a John Fawcett Skelton. I also discovered that for many years young local couples had carried a stone up to that cairn on the moors to seal their own engagement in a kind of tribute to the murdered woman. So a tragic event had transformed into a local tradition. Then judging by the state of the cairn when I first saw it, and probably just as slowly, it had all begun to fade away and disappear back into the moorland.

Skelton's ballad was full of mannered imagery, but it was still evocative, and included the appearance of a guardian angel and the devil, along with sparks flying from the clog irons of the fleeing murderer. I reckoned it would make a starting point for a theatre event, and we could give both the cranky old ballad and the story of Ellen Strange a new lease of life. I asked my friend Don McKinlay if he would carve a stone that could be sunk deep into the moorland next to the cairn. A simple thing I imagined, one that might look old from its beginning. Mid-Pennine Arts provided a small grant, and I persuaded the local Council Parks Department to help by providing a tractor to haul the stone up to the site. I telephoned John Whittaker (who had recently formed Peel Holdings – Peel Tower is a close neighbour to Ellen Strange) to ask him to allow us to take a suitably large stone from one of his quarries. Of course he didn't know who I was but, after a certain amount of pestering, he let me select a large stone from Scout Moor.

Above: Rossendale Carnival, Bacup 1978. Right: At the Bridge Inn, Ewood Bridge 1978

Preparation

I devised a simple scenario inspired by the ballad, and asked Max Bullock, a trumpeter then studying Fine Art at Manchester Art College, to join me along with a group of my students from the Foundation Course, where I was lecturing part-time. Max was a mature student and had already lived several lives. He had learned his instrument in a military band, but by now was a member of a sharp be-bop quartet. He agreed and so I asked a couple of friends I knew from my recent work with the Welfare State theatre group to join us. They included Keith Bray, a crazy and often inspired multi-instrumentalist who went on to work with Horse & Bamboo for several years. We were fortunate in having a singer among the student group – Gail Klevan, now a successful London-based jewellery designer.

Our group spread the word by touring local pubs with a small show that included a new arrangement of the Ellen Strange ballad sung by Gail. I made linocut posters advertising the event, and pasted them on walls and lampposts around the village. A lot of heavy equipment needed to be carried up to the moors, such as the telephone poles which formed the support for two large puppet figures. There was also a field kitchen complete with oven and butane cylinders. Getting this done became the biggest headache of all and in soaked desperation on one particularly wet June day, I jumped into the road and flagged down an army truck full of squaddies (there was a military training camp and firing range on the moorland above the cairn). The bemused sergeant heard me out and, much to my surprise, agreed to load all of our equipment onto their truck and take it up to the site of our ceremony, way up on the moors.

Then, a week or so before Midsummer's Night when the event was due to happen, I was driving home and glimpsed a billboard for the local weekly newspaper outside the newsagent. The headline read "Petition Against Murder Ceremony", or something similar. It took a few seconds for the message to sink in before I stopped the car and went back to pick up a copy. The front page story said that a local woman had created a petition to stop the Ellen Strange event. She felt it celebrated murder.

Asking around, I discovered that the petitioner was part of the congregation of St. Thomas's Church in Helmshore. I went to see her, but she was unmoved by my suggestion that rather than commemorating a murder the event would help to preserve a local story that in turn was part of our heritage. That it no more encourages murder than Easter Eggs encourage crucifixions. But she did suggest that I should have a word with the vicar. This I did, and thankfully he received me sympathetically. He promised to talk to the petitioner and her immediate circle and, a few days later, his secretary phoned me to say that we would hear no more about petitions, and the event could go ahead with their blessing.

The Ceremony

At 10pm on June 24th 1978, a performance, *The Ballad of Ellen Strange*, and the unveiling of a carved memorial stone took place at the cairn of Ellen Strange. It was based on Fawcett Skelton's Victorian ballad. It was not, as some people have since suggested, a 're-enactment' of the murder of Ellen Strange. 55 people trekked up to the moors to join the company at the site of the cairn. Surrounding it was an outer circle of black and white woodcut banners fluttering on bamboo poles; each banner was printed with one word and an image taken from the ballad.

In the centre, supported by the telegraph poles, were two huge puppet figures – one of a woman, the other of a man. Between these and the banners were four coloured 'stations', each depicting a verse from the ballad. The event started with a masked traveller appearing on the old moor-top footpath from Edgeworth, approaching the cairn from the east. The musicians then moved in an anticlockwise direction, stopping at each 'station' where Gail would sing one of the reworked verses from Skelton's Ballad. Finally the carved stone was unveiled as we approached midnight. Everyone was then offered a hot devil-shaped loaf and mulled blood-red wine from the moorland kitchen, which had been built against the drystone wall; next to the solitary thorn bush, a hundred metres to the north.

This was the first Horse & Bamboo show.

The Cairn and Stone

Today Ellen Strange's memorial and cairn are marked on the large-scale OS map of the area. The site has also become a place for an annual pilgrimage, supported by the Unite union, to remember victims of domestic violence. My idea of creating a theatre event to help keep an old story alive, this time at least, had been effective.

12

2. HORSE-DRAWN THEATRE

I don't remember exactly when the idea of using horses and carts to take theatre shows around the country first crossed my mind. It must have been soon after the Ellen Strange event in 1978 when I was still looking for a way of bringing new audiences to theatre. I knew next to nothing about horses, but I wondered if a horse-drawn theatre would attract rural audiences in a way that vans or trucks never would. Maybe it was an idea that would stir folk memories? Perhaps it would trigger images of strolling players and bring people out to watch a show, even though the performances themselves might be strange and unfamiliar?

From 1975 to 1977 I worked with *Welfare State* (later *Welfare State International*) and saw some wonderful work taken to rural venues, only for shows to be cancelled because of the lack of an audience. I guessed that people simply didn't turn up to see something that seemed unfamiliar to them. As I began to look more closely at how the logistics of a horse-drawn tour might work, it occurred to me that meeting up with people in advance of a tour whilst looking for suitable routes and arranging the necessary grazing and camping, might also help us to make friends and connect with a potential audience.

In truth, at this time I had relatively little experience of theatre. But the two years I had spent with Welfare State had given me confidence, and working in performance seemed more and more like a natural development from my work as a painter and printmaker.

Above: The Horse & Bamboo wagon, Hungary, 1993
Right: Travelling in Hertfordshire, 1982

Touring with horses

From the beginning, travelling with horses had a big effect on every part of our work and practice. We needed to ask performers to sign up for a whole tour, 7 days a week, as the horses required our complete commitment. Clearly we couldn't just decide to go away and leave them for a few days. We would try to accommodate emergencies that entailed someone leaving us for a night or two, but equally we couldn't make any promises. Routes had to be reconnoitred months ahead, usually by myself with the horse-handler. We also noted suitable places for tea-breaks, grazing stops, and overnight stays. These were all entered into a tour diary as part of the reconnaissance, and any necessary permissions would then be found, ideally while we were still out on the reccy.

Usually the performers would walk (sometimes run) alongside or behind the carts, or drays. Each travel day we walked between 6 and 16 miles – rarely less, sometimes more. The routine we aimed for was a show day alternating with a travel day, and one day off in seven – this way we managed three shows a week. Occasionally we would perform at a venue for longer than one night, but this was an untypical occurrence, though always welcomed. Everyone involved was super fit by the end of a tour.

On the whole it was a very successful model. Walking, cooking, camping and working as a company really brought a group of performers together, rather like the crew of a ship. All of this spilled over into our theatre practice, and it created strong bonds within the company. It wasn't unusual for us to have a dozen or more people together on the road, each with their own tent. In addition to the performers and horse-handlers our families and friends would often travel along with us. No matter how many people were on the road, horse-drawn touring generally seemed to bring everyone closer together.

Managing horses

We started out with one horse and a donkey. A friend in London, Win Hunt, had a horse and wanted to move out of the capital. I wrote to Win, and eventually went down to meet her and discuss the situation. Within a few days she agreed to leave London and move up to Rossendale. With her she brought her horse, Boot, plus Mingus the donkey who came along with his own special cart.

Over the years each horse-handler became a central part of the company. Win, then Jay Venn, Moira Hirst, Ele Wood, Barry Lee, Liam Carroll, Sue Day, Gary Hill, Graham Fell and Glen Wilson all became key figures in our group. For some it was just one tour; others stayed and worked with the company for several years. When they weren't touring they would often be training the horses or on reconnaissance for the next tour. Naturally, each had their own distinctive way of doing the job, and these differences would subtly alter the way the rest of us worked together. Some horse-handlers would occasionally allow the company to ride up on the drays for a few miles, others refused to allow any riding up as a matter of course.

Soon we had three turnouts on the road as part of a tour, and members of the cast would be trained by the horse-handler to get to know the horses and handle the other drays. There was never any shortage of volunteers to take on these extra responsibilities, and the effect on company morale was always positive. A few performers, such as Jill Penny, became almost as expert with our horses as in their roles in the theatre. Two of the carts were flat-beds that carried the bulk of the show; the other was a wagon, made from scratch by Ele Wood. Over the years it would be repainted several times, each with a completely new design. The wagon had a dual role in both advertising the company and the current performance, and provided us with shelter in really bad weather. We also travelled with a back-up van that went ahead to check the routes and the venues, did our shopping, and usually carried the electrical and technical equipment.

Left: Bamburgh Castle, 1983. Above: All Hungary, 1993 except centre left: Caithness, 1992

Right: Woodcut 'Around the chitties', 2023

Left: Puncture on route to Buxton Festival, 1979

Left: Roma women watching our procession, Hungary, 1993

Left: Sarah overtakes a local, Hungary, 1993

3. PICTURES FROM BRUEGHEL, 1979

More and more of my teaching work on the Foundation Course touched on performance and visual theatre. Mala Sikka, a foundation student who had worked on the Ellen Strange event, had gone on to study Theatre Design at Central School in London. She remained in touch and told me about the work she was doing in her first year at college, including a new project led by Peter Schumann. Schumann is the founder of the influential Vermont-based *Bread & Puppet Theatre*. He was bringing a Bread & Puppet show, *Masaccio*, from the USA and was looking for local musicians to help out. Mala asked if our Horse & Bamboo musicians would take part.

When I eventually went down to London to see what was going on I was surprised to see that the Masaccio project appeared to be an almost entirely visual event. Peter Schumann's students were making clay reliefs based on Masaccio's frescoes, casting from them, and then painting the resulting panels. Masaccio was an early Renaissance painter – one of the first realist artists. I learned that the material Peter used for making these panels was called celastic. This is a resin impregnated cloth that was widely used in theatre at that time to make strong durable props. It's no longer used as the process requires the liberal use of acetone, which we now know is highly toxic.

The handmade *Masaccio* images were duplicated over and over and hung in vertical rows, creating visual backdrops for the performance. Celastic was also used to make the masks. The whole thing looked great, and the performance itself was loose and casual, held together by the presence of Schumann, narrating and playing fiddle and percussion. When Peter Schumann left London I inherited his left over celastic sheets, some acetone, and a few ideas.

It all kicked off in 1979 with *Pictures From Brueghel*, a show that was adapted and redesigned at every venue. Bearing in mind my experience at *Welfare State*, I decided to hedge my bets. There would be no fixed theatre space beyond a few cloth screens, and no tickets or charge of any kind for the audience, who could therefore come and go as they pleased. It took place within an open landscape, adapting to the features of each venue (which would usually be the town park).

Pictures From Brueghel, based on the life of the 16th century Flemish painter Pieter Brueghel, was told largely by recreating images from his paintings. It was essentially a visual experience, with live music, and there were few words. I've always had a love/hate relationship with words and a caution about speech, and this approach served us well, and for the next 35 years our shows remained essentially visual, using a minimum of words. Breughel remains popular for his paintings of wide-screen landscapes populated with characters acting out proverbs, children's games, and similar. I had also discovered the Brueghel poems of Williams Carlos Williams at this time, and loved the way that they described things in such straight-forward language. An idea was to make our own Brueghel-inspired celastic panels on stakes and set them into the landscape, performing in the spaces between them.

Pictures From Brueghel was our first ever tour. But before that, in June 1979, we had a week-long residency at Chester Arts Centre. In Chester we took over the whole centre, making and rehearsing the show and the music in a large public gallery, hugely influenced by *Masaccio*, the Bread and Puppet residency and show that I had seen at the Central School in London.

The story opened with most of the cast playing an overture on hand-made bamboo instruments; our instruments arranged in rows on the grass. Into this scene a mother enters, carrying the baby Brueghel. Characters from Brueghel's paintings pass by – three blind men leading one another in hooded cloaks and tapping their sticks; a Birdman and other bizarre creatures run through the performing area, which changed from place to place, depending on the landscape we were performing in. Then everything suddenly changes and there's a section of small sideshows, all happening simultaneously so that the audience walks around and chooses what to focus on, and in what order.

The themes are loosely based on the seven deadly sins and seven virtues. The show finishes as everyone comes together again and a procession of beggars lead us back to the bamboo orchestra as a large wicker puppet of the painter is raised. Every member of the audience was given a little book of linocuts that I had made. It was called 'The Little World' and brought together images of Brueghel's 7 Deadly Sins and the 7 Virtues (see pages 27 and 28).

The horse-drawn tour itself circumnavigated Manchester, a journey of roughly 250 miles. We started in Rossendale and Ramsbottom in mid-July, and then headed south for Buxton Festival.

Above: The Bamboo Band at the opening of the show

This was also memorable as the place where we had our first ever horse-drawn puncture. The AA (Automobile Association) relayed us, horse, donkey, carts and all, into the town park. Not only that, but they then generously took the whole company out for a sit-down curry, and paid for it (see page 19).

In early August we moved east to Frodsham; then north to Blackpool. Here we camped in the grounds of the zoo for two weeks, as the town council were attempting to remove travellers from a number of sites in the town, and were concerned that lawyers for the travelling families might use granting us permission to camp on public land as a legal precedent. Still, the zoo was a wonderful base for us. The Director, Cyril Grace, gave me the keys so we could let ourselves in and out at night. Mr Grace was a colourful host who kept a collection of rare malt whiskies in the zoo's cellars. On the reconnaissance visits he had regaled me with stories of his friendly rivalry with Gerald Durrell, and the importance of designing the animal enclosures around an intimate knowledge of the sexual habits of each species.

After this we moved on to Bolton Festival during the last week of August, including a parade with Fred Dibnah, who followed us on one of his traction engines. Throughout we performed and camped in parks and other rural public spaces. It was a fabulous experience.

Above: Celastic panels decorating the performance area

Top: Wandering Brueghel character in Buxton Park
Below: Bob Frith at Chester Arts Centre
Over page: The Little World book hand printed and given to the audience

4. THE HOME-MADE CIRCUS, 1980

The next year, with *The Home-Made Circus*, we made a simple tented circular space, open to the sky, which allowed us to charge a small entrance fee.

One of the big influences at this time was a group of young artists from Leiden, Netherlands, who worked together under the name *Matrogoth*. It was Frank Berbee who introduced them to me. Frank was sixteen when I first met him; he had left school and hitch-hiked to France in order to find work with *Welfare State* in Lille.

Frank didn't stay long with *Welfare State*, but he kept in touch with me and ended up working on the Brueghel show. In 1980 he asked about working again on our second horse-drawn tour. Frank was precocious, playing a range of musical instruments, as well as being a poet, a maker and performer. I had briefly worked with *Matrogoth* in Leiden, and there met other members of the company – Bram Groothof, Ron Peperkamp, Peter Lindhout, and Adriaan Krabbendam among them. These were all skilled and distinctive artists, despite only being in their early 20s. Bram was very tall and thin, a virtuoso keyboard player; Ron wore sabots, and knew a lot about radical theatre practice as well as having a powerful performing presence. Peter was a self-sufficient, thoughtful and practical man, with inspired construction skills. Adriaan was kind, bookish and enigmatic, a choirmaster, and an expert on the Tarot.

We would stay up late discussing and arguing about theatre. The Dutch group had an extremely radical mindset compared to most British performers I had met, and they made me feel cautious by contrast. They pushed boundaries and were prepared to take physical and mental punishment to get what they wanted. We hardly ever entirely agreed on anything, but their energy and attitudes strongly infected my own ideas.

These discussions often centred on the role of the group and evolving ideas together through improvisation, rather than through a lead director or writer. These were new concepts to me as my experience had been of art college, and in taking sole responsibility for my own artwork. So this period was an important one in which I struggled with my role within the context of working as an ensemble.

The show

So the *Matrogoth* group had a big impact on our second touring show, *The Home Made Circus*. Peter Lindhout designed and built a beautiful circular white-cloth tented space, which was decorated with my huge woodcuts. We also liked the fact that at every venue Peter would send everyone off for an hour and erect the theatre entirely by himself.

The show was influenced by the writings of the American West Coast poet Gary Snyder, which we would now describe as an environmental call to arms. We concocted a sort of 'circus' using odd life-size puppet-animals and Snyder's wild, visionary stories of salvation, with Ron as the ring-master. It was a dark, ecological tale built around six scenes, which portrayed the devastation which seemed to have been called down by humanity onto the natural world. The Circus itself was, in essence, the circle of the tented space, and in this we met all sorts of creatures including grasses, trees and angels. Man himself was sometimes a Workman, sometimes a Wolf. Despite its bleak subject, the show was well received and we had good audiences, many of them ordinary people from the housing estates in the mill-towns that we passed through. My big hope for horse-drawn touring seemed to be working.

Managing things

Horse & Bamboo had by now grown into an entourage of over a dozen people, which included our own top-hatted chef, Sam Richardson. At this stage we had no specialist administration, which was undertaken by myself with help from a few of the others, with a few hours being put aside each week to manage budgets and deal with bookings. By today's standards this might seem wildly impractical but it was, in fact, perfectly possible to run a reasonably well organised company this way. One big advantage was that nearly all of our small income could be spent directly on making shows and paying the performers.

At the year end we had a deficit almost exactly equalling the grants we had received. Meaning that we had spent twice what we earned. Fortunately most of this was paid off with an end of year one-off grant from North West Arts. I was still lecturing at the art college and was able to cover the final outstanding amount from my own earnings. At this time, Horse & Bamboo's finances were simply being handled through my personal bank account.

In addition to touring with *The Home-Made Circus* the company took part in the Wolverhampton Festival of Performance, and held an exhibition and a number of other events at the Bluecoat Gallery in Liverpool. We also participated in various local community activities.

But there was no doubt that with all the excitement about new and radical theatre ideas, we had spent too little time on the booking side of things. The organisation of the tour suffered, and the tour of *The Home-Made Circus* ended up being a rather short and local one. It was on the road for just over a month, in which time we took it to Rossendale, Ramsbottom, Accrington, and Padiham, albeit with trips out to St.Helens and Manchester.

Everyone at that time was paid the same; a flat rate of £50 a week while working on the show (equivalent to just over £200 a week in 2023). That same year we received a grant from North West Arts of £2840. Receiving funding from the London-based Arts Council or the regional arts bodies was almost essential for a company to survive and prosper. Very few arts companies were able to avoid this. At the time the policies of the Arts Council were far more artist-centred than they become a decade later. The arts officers we knew in 1980 took a personal interest in all of their clients, would frequently visit, and would always come to see a new production. We also received a fee from each place we visited, normally from the local authority.

5. LITTLE HEADS (SHOULDN'T WEAR BIG HATS), 1981

Three years in, and I was now renting a workshop in Irwell Vale which was large enough to accommodate a company of twelve or more. It was extremely basic, with no running water, and a chemical loo in a lean-to among the trees outside. We had one large wood-fired stove to heat the place, which was an old pump house that had originally powered the now derelict village mill. Most of the company slept on the racks that had been built to store fabric and wood. But despite the lack of facilities the feeling within the group was positive, with a constant state of excitement and buzz about all the possibilities we imagined we could see ahead of us.

The next show, in 1981, was *Little Heads (Shouldn't Wear Big Hats)*, and I decided to add a covered seating area to the touring performance space that would give the audience some protection from rain.

Perhaps because of the move to a new workshop, or the effort and focus going into the development and building of the performing space, somehow the script for a new show was left to the last minute, and much of it was developed through improvisation. The Dutch artists had, by and large, now returned to Leiden, and they had been great believers in developing theatre shows this way. But no matter, as a result the production suffered badly. Clearly improvisation wasn't something that worked well for me, or for the group that had gathered at the new workshop. I was still uncertain about what my exact role within Horse & Bamboo should be, but the unpreparedness around the production galvanised me into seeing that it had to be my job as the director of the company to make certain that we were always properly prepared, and I never again allowed such a situation to develop.

Above: Street performance, Burnley town centre, 1981

The script, such as it was, was once again based around writings by the poet Gary Snyder, who had been the inspiration for *The Home-Made Circus*. One of its strong points was an interlude with Edward Taylor, using his own painted story-boards, who told his stories directly to the audience. Edward joined up with another member of the company, Sue Auty, during the tour, and they went on to form the Whalley Range All-Stars, until recently a much loved feature of Manchester's performance scene.

In one way, at least, using improvisation turned out to be of great benefit in developing our street performances. These were ad-hoc affairs that were taken out onto the streets to advertise the main show, and during this tour they really came into their own, frequently possessing an impact that was missing from the main show.

At this point we were invited to take part in Leicester Festival, and I negotiated permission to build our own theatre at Leicester Marina, using scrap wood from old canal boats. It was also an opportunity to totally rework the show and add elements that had been discovered during the street performances. The Leicester Festival show was a triumph, and became one of the hits of the festival. On the last night, we led the audience out of the canal-side venue, and then burned our theatre to the ground.

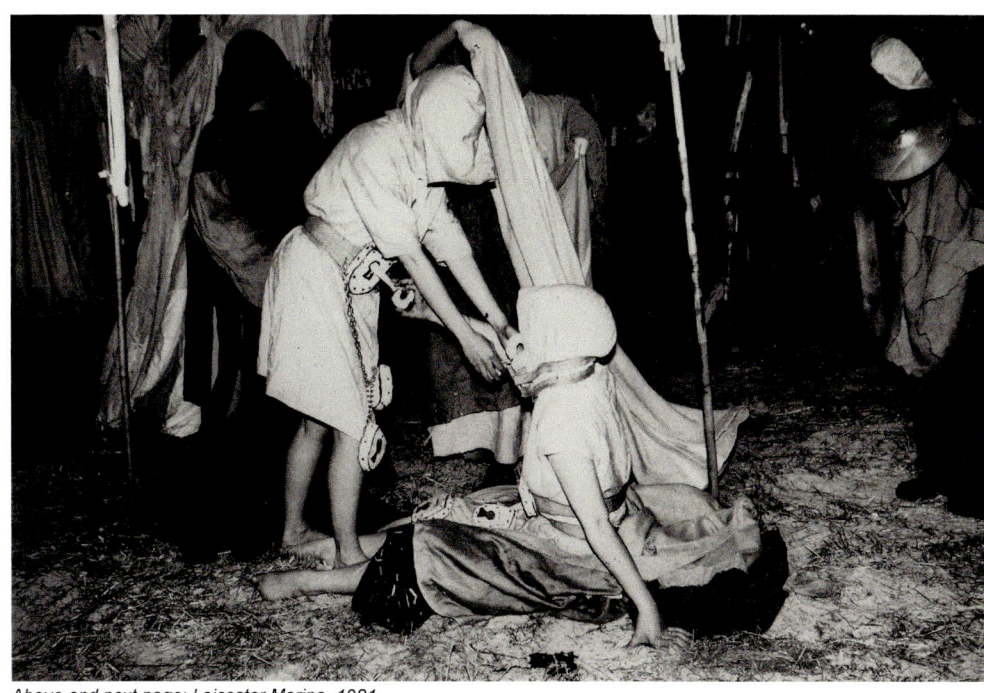

Above and next page: Leicester Marina, 1981

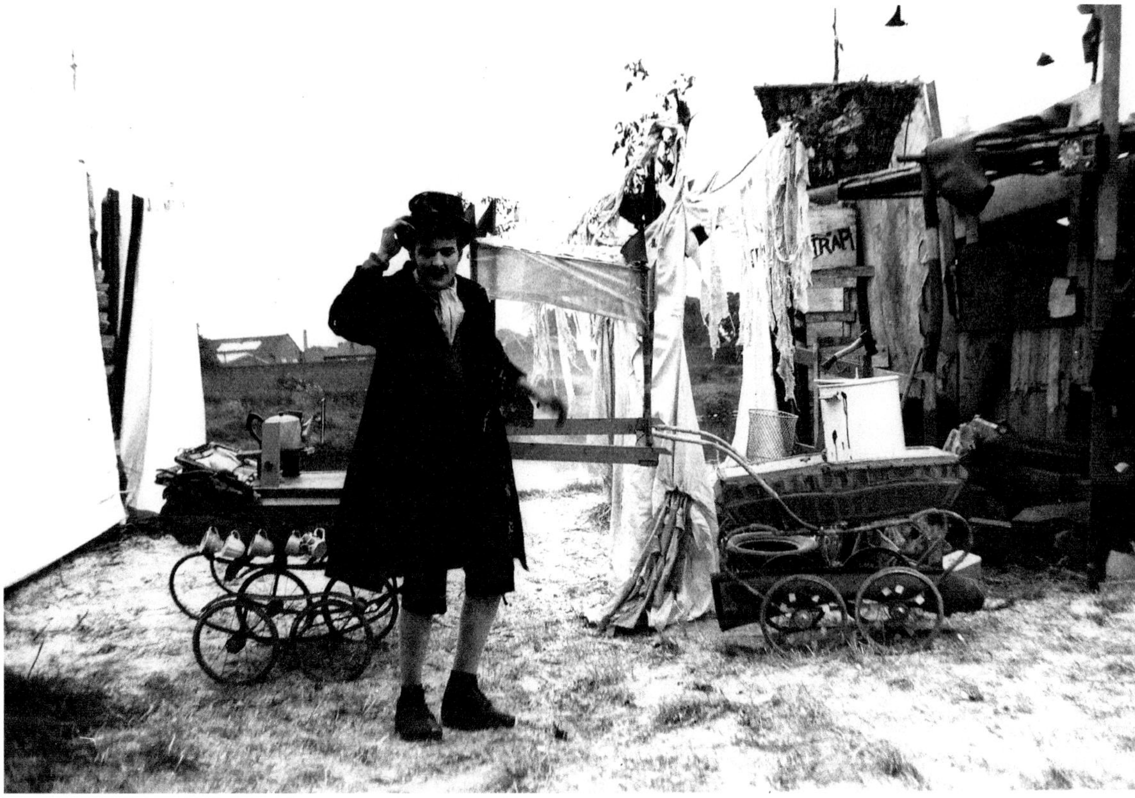
TRAP

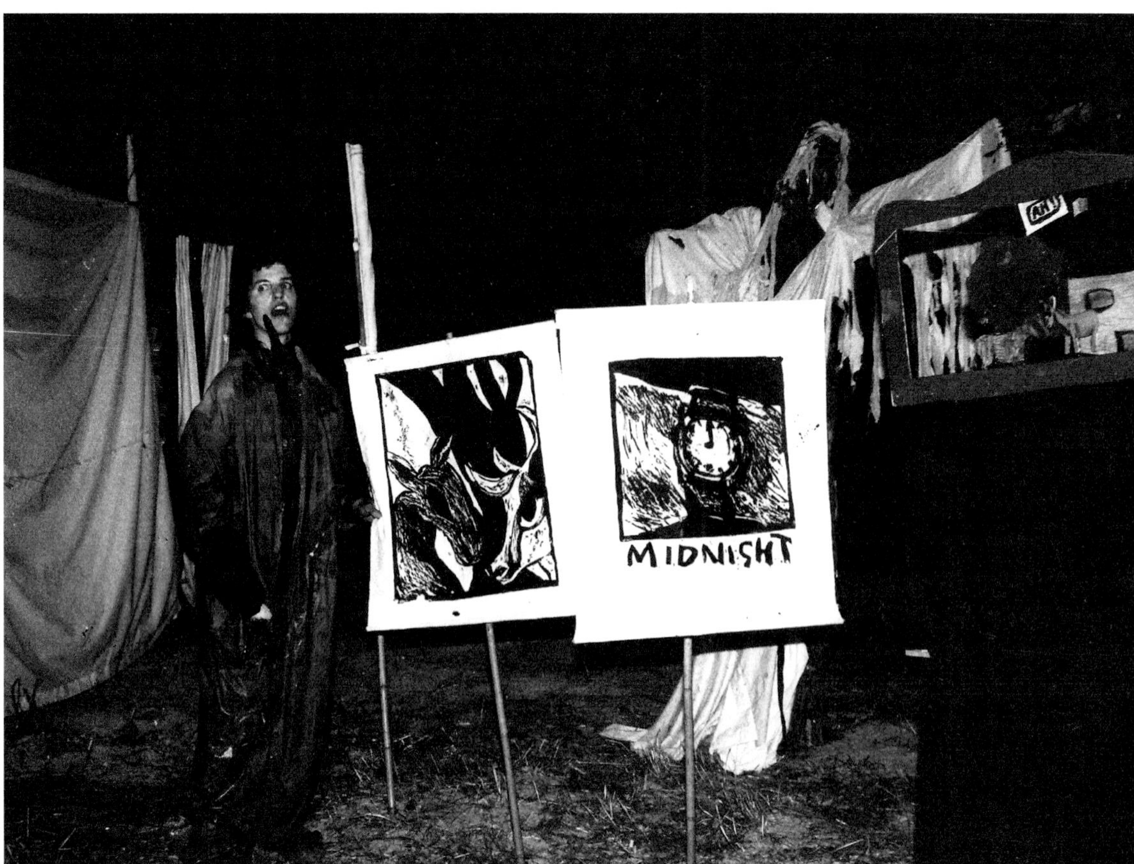
MIDNIGHT

6. THE WOODCARVERS STORY, 1982

My family moving from Stoke Newington in north London to Stevenage in 1956 was a huge change for me. In Stevenage we lived on the edge of town, and in two minutes I could be in the countryside. It meant that a lot of my free time was taken up exploring the fields, streams, ponds and dells – all within walking distance. As I grew older I ventured further and further from home. Three miles away, in a village called Woolmer Green, I came across the house of an elderly wood-carver. Later I discovered that his name was Harry Macdonald and that he was, originally, from Bradford.

During the Depression of the 1930s Harry had walked south down the A1 looking for work. When he arrived at Woolmer Green he found a barn for rent. He decided to stay, selling wood-carvings to travellers along the Great North Road. He soon realised that it would help if he created something sufficiently eye-catching to stop the traffic by his workshop.

The house and garden

Over the next few years Harry covered his workshop in brightly carved figures, including a carved policeman by the side of the road holding up its hand in a 'halt' command. He made the barn into an extraordinary place, a kind of fairytale world. The garden was transformed into a nursery-rhyme village, complete with puppet-like working parts. A cow jumped over a moon. 230 scottie dogs wearing bow-ties ran round the walls of the house. Carved giraffes and toucans looked down onto the road. A witch flew past the chimney on her broomstick. You could turn a handle and a pink elephant would blow water from its trunk. There was a model of the Holy Land too, but it didn't have moving parts and so I thought it much less interesting.

Mr Macdonald was usually to be found around the house, normally in his workshop. He seemed to me to be rather grumpy, which I now recognise as a droll northern manner. Grumpy or not, he could always be relied on to open the peacock gates to his garden. First you had to drop a few pennies into a slide mechanism at the entrance. It would transport the coins straight through the garden and the workshop window into his big hands. I could then wander around, amazed and transported into a storybook world, with Harry's mournful, suspicious gaze checking on me from his grubby window.

Four years after setting up Horse & Bamboo, I was still trying to figure out how the company would work best. Most of my concerns focused around my own role. I supposed that conventionally a theatre director had a script written by a playwright, and took on the responsibility of shaping it through actors and designers, into a play. But the people who inspired me, who had established the theatre groups that I was most affected by, didn't work like that. Instead, they took on the same responsibility as a painter or sculptor. Which meant conceiving and designing theatre events themselves, and then working with others to put it in front of an audience. The *Matrogoth* idea of a communal, more improvised, model had further confused things, but my experience with the near disaster of our previous show, *Little Heads (Shouldn't Wear Big Hats)*, clarified things for me. Once I recognised this, the idea of telling Harry Macdonald's story immediately felt right. It was personal to me, and his life and the puppet-like quality of his work seemed to lend itself to my visual approach. There was another big change too. We invested in an ex-army marquee and, for the first time, our touring shows would be performed inside. The tent made for an enormously atmospheric venue which more than made up for the extra work of erecting it at each venue.

I started looking further into Harry's life and found that he had died in 1971. So I visited Woolmer Green to find out what had happened to his house and its garden. Driving up from London with a friend, I arrived just as it was getting dark. We found the house easily enough, however the carvings that had covered it like a decorative pie crust had disappeared entirely. On closer inspection I found that just two cement scottie dogs remained, forlornly hanging from the walls. The garden was worse – it was now a wasteland that had been bulldozed into oblivion. It must have been done recently as a handful of his carvings were still peeping out of the earth. We quickly grabbed a few of them, hoping not to be caught, then drove away north. Interestingly, there is now a blue plaque on that old barn, which eventually became Harry's house.

38

Back to Woolmer Green

I discovered that, against the wishes of most of the village community, a distant relative of Harry Macdonald had instructed their agent to destroy the garden and strip the property clean in order for it to be sold more easily. In my script of The Woodcarver Story the final scene is of a bulldozer destroying the set. In the old ex-army marquee the puppets and structures that re-created Harry's house and garden were fixed in the ground of the stage area with bamboo poles. As the almost life-size puppet bulldozer moved through the tent all of these were pushed flat and the grass and earth stage area was left as a scene of devastation.

Paul Kershaw played the main Harry Macdonald perfectly, but other members of the cast also took the role, as we saw the Woodcarver slowly age as he constructs his cottage and garden. Fittingly, Paul was himself from Bradford. The horse-drawn tour covered the 200 or so miles from Scunthorpe to Woolmer Green. We stopped at various points to do pre-planned shows en route, including Alford and Digswell House in Welwyn. But the final shows were held in Woolmer Green itself, and our marquee was pitched just a hundred yards from Harry Macdonald's old house. The realisation that the whole tour was a pilgrimage properly dawned on us as our convoy of horses, carts and people slowly moved south towards the Woodcarver's Cottage.

A final performance

At the end of the very last show I beat a large drum, and with the other musicians we led the masked performers, followed by the audience, out of the show-ground. We turned left along the old Great North Road right past the site of Harry's house, and then left again into the village churchyard. Here we made our way to Harry Macdonald's grave. We stopped by the graveside and lit candles; we placed tiny puppet versions of his house and carvings on the tombstone. Our band played one last tune, and a stilt-dancer moved among the gravestones in the cemetery. Then it was over.

When we were leaving the next day, meeting up without horse-transport to take everything back to Lancashire, I met a few of the villagers to thank them for their support. They presented me with a wooden head of a dog, beautifully carved by Harry, as a memento of our visit to Woolmer Green. It's still hanging outside my studio, and I decorate it every Christmas.

Right: Local newspaper photograph showing demolition of Harry Macdonald's garden.

A step forward

In retrospect, *The Woodcarver Story* was a big development in the company's theatre style. Before *The Woodcarver* our shows had combined puppets, objects, music and masks in a loose, surreal and episodic mixture. This approach was influenced by the work I had seen at *Welfare State*, combined with the little I knew of *Bread and Puppet's* work in the US. *The Woodcarver Story* introduced a new, more personal, approach. It remained a visual experience with live music, but added realistic masked characters combined with puppet elements to tell a story that had a more tightly scripted narrative. It was the first Horse & Bamboo show to do this, and the first show in which the company's distinctive, mask-based, style began to emerge. For me it was also the show when I began to feel comfortable in the role of artistic director.

I learned to slow things down. I noticed that performers needed to slow their gestures and actions when performing in masks. Movements had to be extremely deliberate and clear, not blurred or overlapped as they often are in day-to-day activity. Only then was it possible to articulate the thoughts and motivations of characters who didn't have the ability to use words to express their intentions. I also discovered the importance of expressing in the clearest possible way everything that happens on stage – the performing and puppetry, music, any incidental sounds, imagery and movements – with an awareness of what the overall picture is intended to convey to the audience, even when that meaning is meant to be ambiguous. Some of this was considered well beforehand and became part of the writing process. Other parts evolved during the rehearsal. However it came about it was essential to keep the audience actively engaged and thinking; to make every second of the story interesting and challenging in precisely the same way a good storyteller captivates the listeners clustered at their feet, hanging on every word of their story...

REVIEW:

"….This is clarity achieved by working through challenging contrasts. Popular content is conveyed through environmental experimentation. Humble events are told with a mightily fierce expression and tragedy lies side by side with a celebration of beauty. Inanimate artefacts come alive through the animation of human performers. A sense of living and developing tradition runs through their work….."

"The living sculptures of masks and the painted images of the setting reveal a strong link with the tradition of expressionist art that runs from the medieval drawings of Grunewald to this century's glowing colours of Georges Rouault. Among the stylistic influences is an eloquent simple style carrying a greater emotional impact than could be achieved through naturalism. The grasp of traditional art forms is such that the incorporation of of a time based element becomes essential to sustain the concern for story that is at the heart of H&B's work"

Phil Hyde, Performance magazine. Dec/Jan 1983.

Above: Woodcut print, loosely based on performing the Woodcarvers Story in the company marquee, 2023

7. THE WHITWORTH HORSE, 1982

I had a painting studio in the small Rossendale village of Irwell Vale, and in 1978 it became the base for the new theatre company. Over the next year we added an office and a workshop in the pump house, all within the same small village. It remained that way until we moved to Rawtenstall in 1985. Our touring work at this point was limited to the spring and summer months, which left over half the year, September through to March, for the company to do other work.

Irwell Vale was a small village of about 40 houses, and unusual in that it had only one road joining it to the outside world, so it was a self-contained community with its own strong character. Having a theatre company suddenly basing itself in the village, with horses, wagons, and a multi-national membership, made a considerable impact on the community.

It was only natural that we felt it important to give something back to the village, to support and help with various community events. From 1979 we helped organise a November 5th bonfire on the village green. People would bring fireworks, parkin, treacle toffee, or hot dogs. We would design and build the fire and a performance that included live music. These were informal and enjoyable events that just about everyone took part in. The audience eventually grew from the 100 or so villagers living in Irwell Vale to several hundred people flocking into the village by the mid-1980s.

Living and working in a small community there was no alternative but to enter into its inner and outer life. In return we were naturally included in daily village life and appreciated for what we were and what we had to offer. People seemed to enjoy our daily sorties out, training the horses, practising working with the drays, and music rehearsals with the band.

The Irwell Vale workshop initially lacked both power and drainage. We dug a trench and installed our own power line. Drainage was more difficult and so we built a privy behind the redbrick workshop. We took advantage of the fact that the municipal sewage works was only half a mile away and carried the chemical toilet there whenever it was full, driving it there in my old Moskovitch and, when desperate, emptying it by hand into the tanks.

This page: Community bonfires, Irwell Vale, 1980
Previous page: Parade at The Horse Fair, Whitworth, 1982
Following page: Woodcut, Irwell Vale, 1980

HORSE & BAMBOO · IRWELL VALE 1980

Whitworth

Another nearby event was the annual horse-fair in Whitworth, at the other end of the Rossendale Valley. We got to know Walter Lloyd, the de facto squire of Whitworth, through Barbara Laishley (later Vijayakumar). Barbara was born in Whitworth and she had formed *Centre Ocean Stream*, a dance company influenced by Kathakali. Barbara was trained at the Kerala Kalamandalam, from which she graduated in 1976 as the first female and non-Indian Kathakali make-up artist in the world. She also had a great love of horses.

Among many things, Walter had a herd of wild fell ponies that roamed freely on the moorland above his farm. He encouraged the travelling community to camp on his land in Whitworth centre for a week or so every year. The period of the fair was spent racing horses up and down the roads, buying and selling, music round the campfires after dark, and usually a few fist-fights. Understandably some of this alarmed the locals but, on the whole, each year the event passed in a relatively good humoured manner. Horse & Bamboo were encouraged by Walter to take part and so we took to camping there. We would bring our current street shows and, later, the marquee and our summer show.

We got to know many of the travelling families at Whitworth, but our connections with the travelling community weren't limited to the horse-fair. Ever since the decision to use horses as part of our theatre work we had been helped and supported by travellers and their families. Bernard Lyle, who lived in Colne, was especially generous and for several years he found us horses, tack, transport and wagons whenever we needed them. Always accompanied by his generous and cheeky humour and gallons of sweet tea (thank you Marge). Later Brian Laidlaw, along with Rosie and their family, sea-coalers from Spennymoor on the Durham coast, travelled all over Britain with us, taking our horses, wagons and shows to whatever place was the starting point for a new tour, or living on-site, guarding whatever installation we were building.

In 1982 we built a fifty foot high Wooden Horse on the high ground overlooking Whitworth. Because it could only be approached from the steep hill below, it stood against the skyline. It was truly impressive, and people gasped when they saw its silhouette looming on the horizon. On the last night of the Whitworth Fair the Horse & Bamboo band led a torchlit parade up the hill. We went up the track past St. Bartholomew's Church, and there set light to the giant Horse. Whitworth Horse Fair was a stop on the road to Appleby Horse Fair, the largest gathering of travellers in the country. That year they took with them the story of the Giant Burning Horse. It entered traveller legend, and for years after we were often flagged down by people who wanted to talk to us about the burning of the giant wooden horse.

Left: View from Bartholomew's Church, of the building of the horse

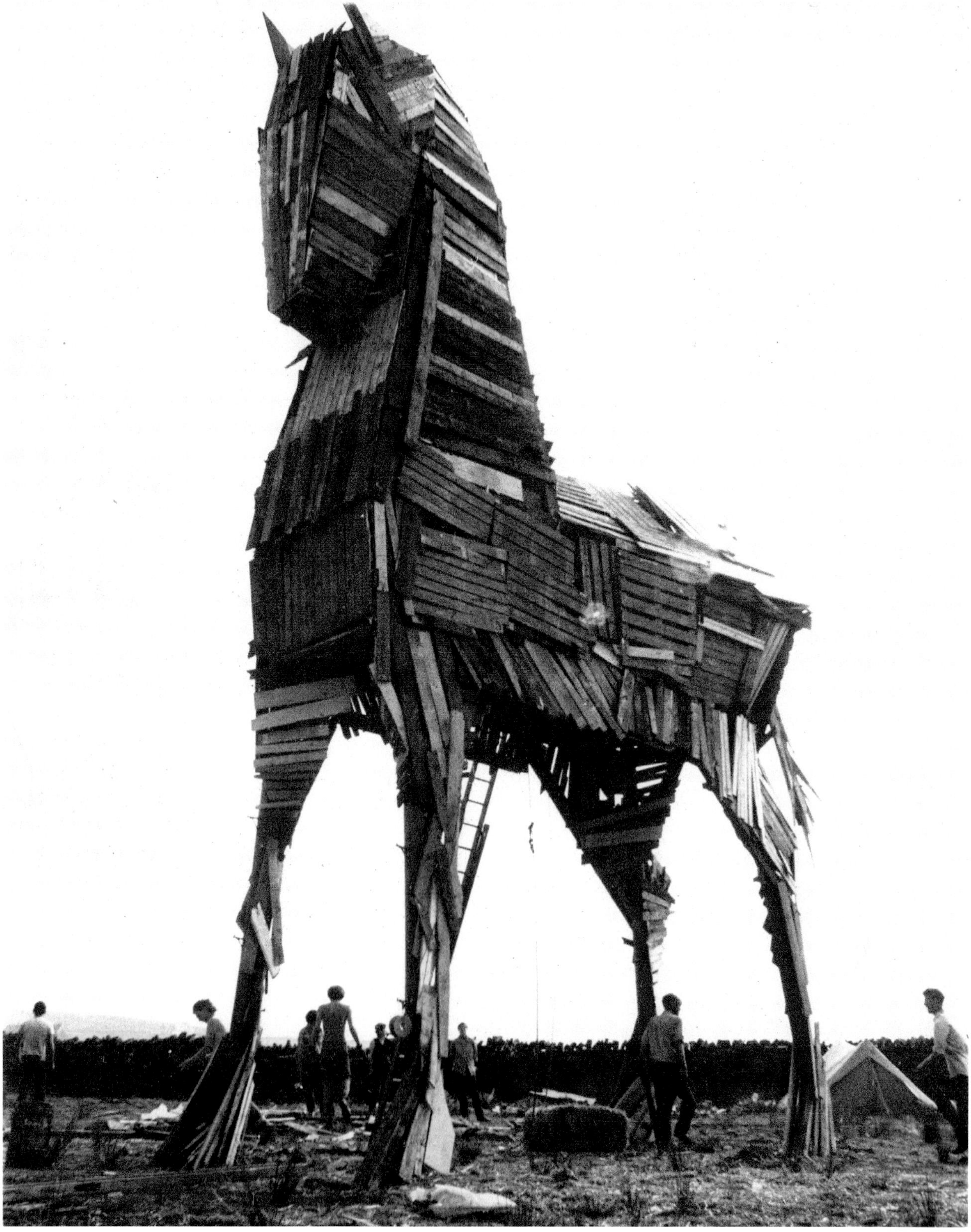

8. GUIDED IMAGERY 1981-2006

In 1981 I received a letter from a teacher who had seen one of our shows at the Manchester Railway Exposition, which is now the Manchester Museum of Science & Industry. The letter explained how as a teacher at a special school, he had been struck by how 'hard-hitting' the masks and archetypal themes we used were. He wondered if 'the combination of visual overkill and massively mythic drama (could) be just the thing to break into the streams of unconscious that typify M.H.' We discussed the letter with Kay Kennedy, who had just graduated from St. Albans as an art therapist. Then together we sat down and discussed what it would mean working within a special school environment.

The 1981 company was cautious about undertaking this. We went through various scenarios – what would work for children who would be emotionally volatile and unpredictable, or were emotionally withdrawn and possibly terrified? Some might be on medication. Others could also have severe physical impairments; blind or deaf, perhaps dependent on wheelchairs…

Ultimately we felt that we really wanted to take up the challenge. The basic format we came up with in 1981 formed the template for a new strand of work for the next 25 years. Work that was challenging, exciting, stimulating, above all enjoyable and sometimes producing amazingly effective results. It became work that was increasingly popular with our team of performers and makers, and our extended family of artists queued to work on these events. A few of our most committed and skilled artists, such as Martin Pearson or Alan Henry, rarely took part in the company's touring shows, but were indispensable to the success of these productions. From the beginning they came to be known collectively as *Guided Imagery*. The projects became increasingly ambitious, and were some of the most successful and groundbreaking events that we ever undertook.

At its simplest the format was to start by welcoming small groups into a safe and comfortable environment. We never talked about anyone visiting the theatre. Instead people came to whatever imaginary world formed the theme and subject for that particular project. We would say that it was a visit to a submarine, a narrowboat, or a space rocket. We went to great lengths to make these spaces believable and realistic. Most of all they needed to be reassuring and friendly spaces.

Then, once everyone was settled, we went on a journey together. The journey was made to be as realistic as possible – the vehicle would be sprung and equipped with a motor, lights and controls. At first all would go well. When we felt that we had gained the group's confidence, and that they trusted us as their guides, something unexpected would happen. In other words there would be an emergency of some kind. So the lights would go out, flash on and off; there would be a jolt, some level of panic and noise. This stage was always very carefully managed, and how far the experience would be taken totally depended on the reactions of each group. All our effects, such as sound and lights, could be modified depending on the particular situation as it unfolded. Of course we had experienced guides on board too, able to respond directly to the participants, one-to-one if necessary.

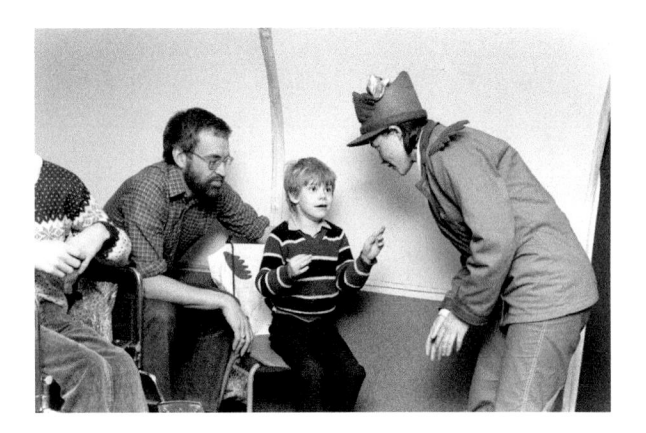

After this crisis the group next had to decide how to deal with the problem. For people who lived in a situation where every decision was usually taken for them by carers, this was often a shock. These were in the days before care-in-the-community, and many of the groups we worked with lived in enormous Victorian hospitals. So a crisis would be genuinely unexpected. Shall we use the emergency door to find our own way back? Can we try and repair the engine? Should we send a volunteer ahead to see how things were outside? It would be an anxious period involving problem solving, group bonding, and sometimes acts of real emotional courage.

During the final stage everybody involved would help resolve the problem, and we could successfully return to normality. Which meant getting back to the starting point, to 'home'. But now there would be an enhanced sense of achievement and self-worth in having overcome the problem. Inevitably this would include a sense of relief and a celebration of what had been achieved together.

These journey sessions would usually last between two and three hours. In most cases, after a lunch period, we then returned to the environment and looked again at the illusory journey. Where appropriate sharing the fact that we had all played a part in a kind of game. This would be followed by a short making, play or acting session.

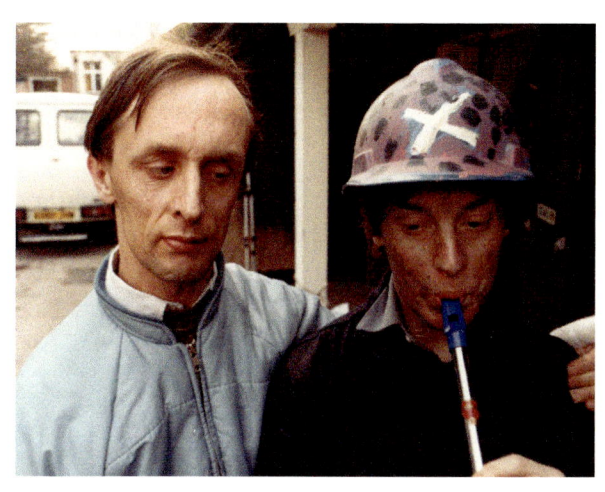

This and previous pages: Selection of photographs from various Guided Imagery shows

50

The environments

The work that went into constructing these complex built environments was enormous. We built the 'vehicles', the safe rooms, and the unsafe worlds that the participants were thrown into. Plus, of course, the 'escape route' out of this world. The *Guided Imagery* environments filled large halls and would take a team of between 6 and 8 artists up to 6 weeks to construct.

On most Guided Imagery projects there would be one group visiting each day. A group would normally consist of 10 participants, plus their carers – 1, 2, 3 or more depending on the make-up of the group. Every space had to be wheelchair accessible, and every environment had to fully controllable by the performers. Our cast also operated the sound and light, and even on occasion introduced appropriate scents that helped create the sense of an actual journey.

Over this 25 year period we created a menagerie, complete with an aquarium, insect house, and underground caves; a flight to the moon; a journey from a water research laboratory to a subterranean lake complex; a haunted shoe shop; a fairground; a window manufacturer; an island; a jungle; a fish and chip shop that led to a trawler which in turn sailed to a desert island and lighthouse; a narrow-boat journey, involving a labyrinth that took us beneath a castle. Each day the show would vary too, as performers responded to the reactions of particular participants, to their fears, their triumphs, their ideas and their own contributions to the journey that we were taking together.

Funding

The *Guided Imagery* events were at first annual, later every two years. Funding was raised mainly from charities and trusts. Each project normally lasted around 6 weeks, and 30 groups would have participated in and benefited from them by the time the project ended.

But they tied up a lot of our resources. With a 6 week building period, followed by 6 weeks of performances, it would mean that our theatre space was out of use for anything else for almost 3 months of the year. At first this wasn't seen as an issue, but during the 1990s the Arts Council of England began increasingly to measure success by counting the numbers of participants rather than the quality of their experience. Most of the old-style arts administrators left, often in frustration, and a new kind of thoroughly business-orientated mentality took over. It became rarer for anybody from the Arts Council to visit to watch a show. It was the statistics that counted. So with our *Guided Imagery* work, working with 300 people over 3 months didn't seem that impressive. No matter how profound that experience had been, or how potentially life-changing it was.

Guided Imagery shows were events in which people who were understood to be mute, who didn't talk, occasionally spoke for the first time. Places where carers and staff would see some of those in their care in a new light, because they observed them respond under real pressure. Places where people who were normally carefully looked after and had few opportunities to show any initiative, might suddenly do something stunningly unexpected. Almost everyone who participated in *Guided Imagery* events came away with a new sense of self-worth. Despite all of this by 2006 it was clear that *Guided Imagery* shows were no longer financially viable.

9. NEEDLES IN A CANDLEFLAME, 1983

Up until now Horse & Bamboo had operated as a kind of spin-off of my work as an artist, but in 1983 it was constituted properly as a company, which we called 'Little World' Ltd. It meant we were expected to have a Board of Trustees, and Walter Lloyd became tour first Chair. That year we were given a significant increase in our grant from the North West Arts Board. The Arts Board at this stage had taken a lot of interest in the development of the company, advising me and nurturing our work. The arts officer responsible for the company, Sally Medlyn, visited us frequently, unafraid to ask hard questions, but also making sure that she saw every new show and project that we produced. Peers from the arts, including the sculptor David Nash and Adrian Henri, the poet and painter, were sent to write reports and recommendations about our work. The extra funding was a direct outcome of this scrutiny, and it meant that we could now tour with a cast of 9, including three musicians. We had also been joined by Adam and Kim Strickson. In addition to being a valued performer and musician, Adam also took on a considerable amount of the administration of the company, and he was the first person to seriously take on this role.

China Men

The 1983 touring show was based very loosely on the story 'On Discovery' from Maxine Hong Kingston's novel 'China Men'. It's the story of a shipwrecked sailor, who finds himself washed up on the shore of the Land of Women. At first, rescued by the inhabitants, he can't believe his luck, and thinks he has fallen on his feet. But then, as he undergoes the routines, restraints, habits and tortures (foot-binding, hair plucking etc) that women endure, he realises that he is slowly and painfully being transformed into a woman himself, and that it's no joke.

We began the show with a 15 minute film, made in a 16mm black-and-white period style. This demonstrated the 'enchanting fantasies' acted out by Victorian magicians on their female assistants. To do this we spent weeks in our workshop painstakingly recreating many of the tricks from the early cinema. Doing this we came across the magician, showman and pioneering film-maker Georges Melies. We used an old Bolex 16mm camera and black and white film stock, sending off each days' rushes and receiving them back from the lab early the next morning.

The film included an Expanding Head trick, then the 'Wandering Jew' made an appearance. In this Adam Strickson appears as a figure travelling through a painted mountainous landscape, starting as a small puppet figure in the distance then bursting into the foreground holding a staff, all burning eyes and wild white beard. Next was the 'Framed Lady' (a woman steps out of the frame of her portrait as the artist dreams lascivious thoughts). Then some levitation tricks and that old favourite, sawing a beautiful woman assistant in half. It ended with the 'Brahmin and the Butterfly', in which a caterpillar turns into a beautiful winged butterfly lady (played by Moira Hirst, our horse-handler). These tricks were either created within the camera, or with the help of a conjuror friend, Bim Mason.

After this the curtain fell inside the marquee to open up the theatre space. The image of the Butterfly Woman gave way to the story of a butterfly hunter who is captured by a small group of women. We follow his travails in a Land of Women. Finally, once the audience had left the marquee, there was a short outdoor puppet show. This was based on a Moomintroll story,'The Fillyjonk Who Believed in Disasters'. In 2007 we radically re-worked this section into Storm in a Teacup.

Selling the tour had been more successful this year; we organised a tour that started in Hebden Bridge, then travelled by truck and horsebox to Scotland, where we toured Dunfermline, Pittenweem, St Andrews, and Kirkaldy. Then south into North-East England and Alnwick, Alnmouth, Amble, Acklington, Ashington, Gateshead, Jarrow, Biddick, Cleveland, Yarm, and ending at Darlington Arts Centre.

Top image: Still from opening 16mm film, Needles in a Candleflame
Lower image: One mask, two performers, Needles in a Candleflame. Mask made by Paul Kershaw

Pittenweem Festival

We promoted this fairly edgy production as a 'family show', something I don't think would be possible today. At the first show at the Festival at Pittenweem, a member of the audience stood up and announced that it was 'disgusting'. Ironically, given the story, he ordered his reluctant wife to leave with him. He then asked the audience to join him in walking out in a mass protest. Nobody moved, but he nevertheless reported us to the police. The police in turn asked Joyce Laing, the Festival Director (and the Art Therapist at Barlinnie prison) to check out the show. As she hadn't yet seen it, Joyce came to the very next performance, and we then waited for her verdict. Which was, 'nae problem'.

For the last night of Pittenweem Arts Festival we improvised a raft with a fire sculpture built onto it. The idea was for it to be lit, then floated out to sea from the harbour after the Carnival Parade – the finale of the week-long festival. Unfortunately that night was unusually still and the sea untypical calm, and the raft refused to leave with the tide. Not wanting to disappoint the crowd Melissa Wyer, one of our company, stripped down to her underwear, jumped into the harbour and towed the raft out to sea, swimming with the rope gripped in her mouth.

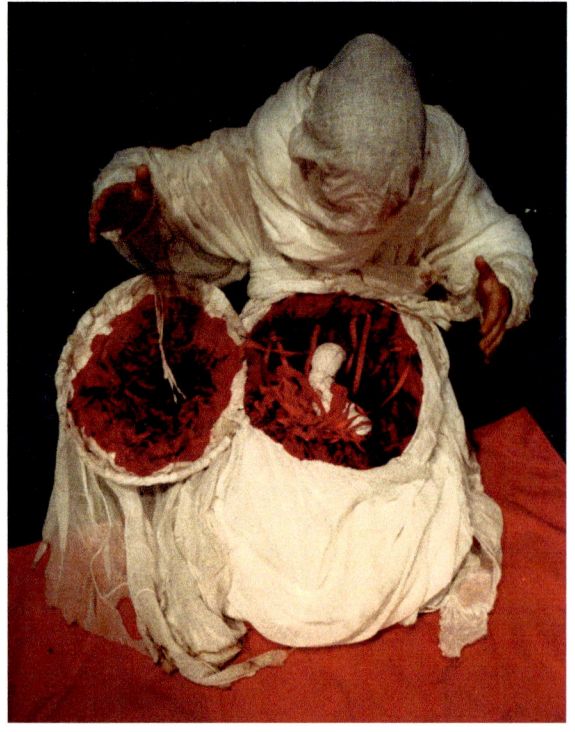

Above left: Image from Needles in a Candleflame
Right: Scene based on the Moomintroll story, from Needles in a Candleflame
Opposite page: Advertising the show at Pittenweem Harbour

55

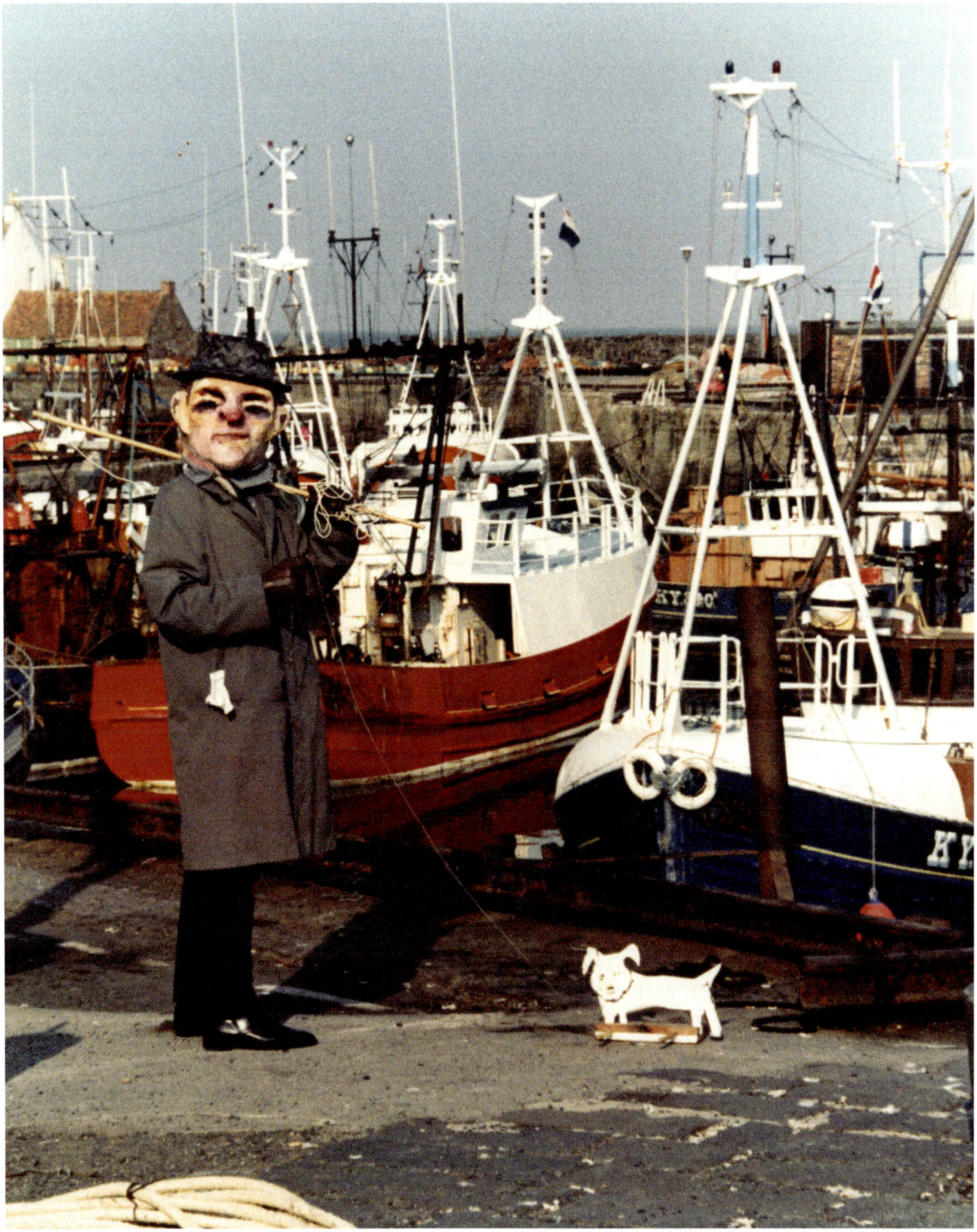
KY

10. SEOL, 1984

Jenny Wilson had been Director at Mid-Pennine Arts and she was a committed supporter of Horse & Bamboo in its early days. It had been Jenny who nurtured my interest in new and radical theatre companies, and who had persuaded Welfare State to base themselves in Burnley in the 1970s. Later Jenny moved on to become Director of the Crawford Arts Centre in St Andrews, and recommended our work to the Scottish Arts Council, who suggested a tour of the Outer Hebrides. So, in October 1983, I went off for a preliminary reconnaissance to see if this attractive possibility would be viable. I began my journey at the southern islands, taking the Calmac ferry from Oban to Barra.

Barra then had a population of about 1200 people, of whom – I was told – only 9 weren't Catholics. It was a Catholic island by virtue of the fact that its remote situation meant that the Reformation had simply never reached it. On arrival I found a room at the Castlebay Hotel and discovered almost immediately that it was also a place that enjoyed a party. In fact I discovered that it seemed to enjoy a party every evening.

Next morning I went down to the Highland and Island Council offices to introduce myself. They were expecting me, but still I explained what I was looking for, namely a flat area of land large enough for us to pitch our marquee. They were enthusiastic, and suggested a few sites for me to go and look at, and then arranged for me to come back the next day so we could move things along. I used the day to explore the island and look at the two pockets of land that were flat and big enough for our marquee. I discovered that Barra was a kind of paradise, with vast, breathtaking beaches, mountain vistas, rolling machair, and plenty of ancient remains. I also took the ferry to Vatersay, the most southerly of the inhabited Outer Islands, with a population of 80.

Everyone I met was extremely helpful and eager to please, but nevertheless I found it strangely difficult to get anything nailed down. When I returned to the council offices on my second morning I reported back on the possible sites for our marquee and there was a lot of nodding and sympathetic murmuring, but trying to pin anything down was impossible. I was beginning to wonder if the idea of a tour to this place was going to be possible when one of the ladies asked if I had seen 'the Father'. Puzzled, I asked who she meant – 'Father Colin', came the reply.

Father Colin

Barra had two priests, one, Father Calum, was based in Castlebay, which is its main settlement and where I was staying; the other was in Northbay at the other end of the island. Father Calum, who also ministered to the Catholics on Eriskay (the next island along the Hebridean chain), was off the island. I phoned and was given an appointment later that day with Father Colin MacInnes, of Northbay parish.

Father Colin was a surprise. I guess that he was about my own age, and clearly a vigorous and charismatic man. When I explained what our intentions would be in coming to Barra he simply asked 'why?', and made me think. Usually when asking whether we could visit and perform for a community, people were immediately charmed by the idea and went out of their way to suggest how it might come to pass. But Fr. Colin wanted to know why. Why did an English theatre company want to come to a Gaelic speaking island with its own, entirely different, culture? Why should money be spent on this rather than on the Gaelic culture that was being left to wither? I had to dig deep that afternoon to reply honestly to his questions.

Father Colin MacInnes turned out to be a leading voice in the fight to reclaim the Gaelic language, both on the Islands and within Scotland in general. He sat on the Board of the Scottish Arts Council and argued passionately for a Gaelic culture that he felt was being ignored. He was also one of the founders of the Fèis movement on the Isle of Barra. These were Barra people who were concerned that local traditions were dying out. At a Fèis individuals come together to develop their skills in Gaelic arts – song, dance, drama, and traditional music on a wide range of instruments. Now Fèisean appear throughout the Gaelic-speaking islands, but in 1983 Father Colin was fighting for the life of his culture. No wonder he was cautious about welcoming me.

In the seventh century Christianity came to Barra, and those early priests and saints, including (possibly) Saint FinnBarr, who gave his name to the island, fought to the death to protect the island and its community. In the old stories they struggled with dragons and serpents, and meeting Father Colin MacInnes that day I saw something still of the priest as a champion, someone who saw their role not just as offering spiritual succour, but a leader who would protect and fight for the community and its way of life, its culture and language.

It was humbling to visit a community for whom the arts meant more than entertainment and diversion. The arts, along with the language, were right at the heart of what defined the place and the community. It reminded me of why rescuing the Ellen Strange story had been important at the beginning of our own story as a theatre company. It didn't surprise me, years later, to hear that Father Colin had moved to Ecuador and fought for his new community against the gang-bosses who intimidated, threatened and stole from them. At one point, I read, he only escaped death at the door of his church by parishioners forming a human shield around him.

I didn't know what to expect next. But when I opened the door to the council offices the following day, my third morning on Barra, there were wide smiles and a completely new approach. Addresses and telephone numbers were handed me, and very quickly a week's stay on Barra for the next summer was sorted.

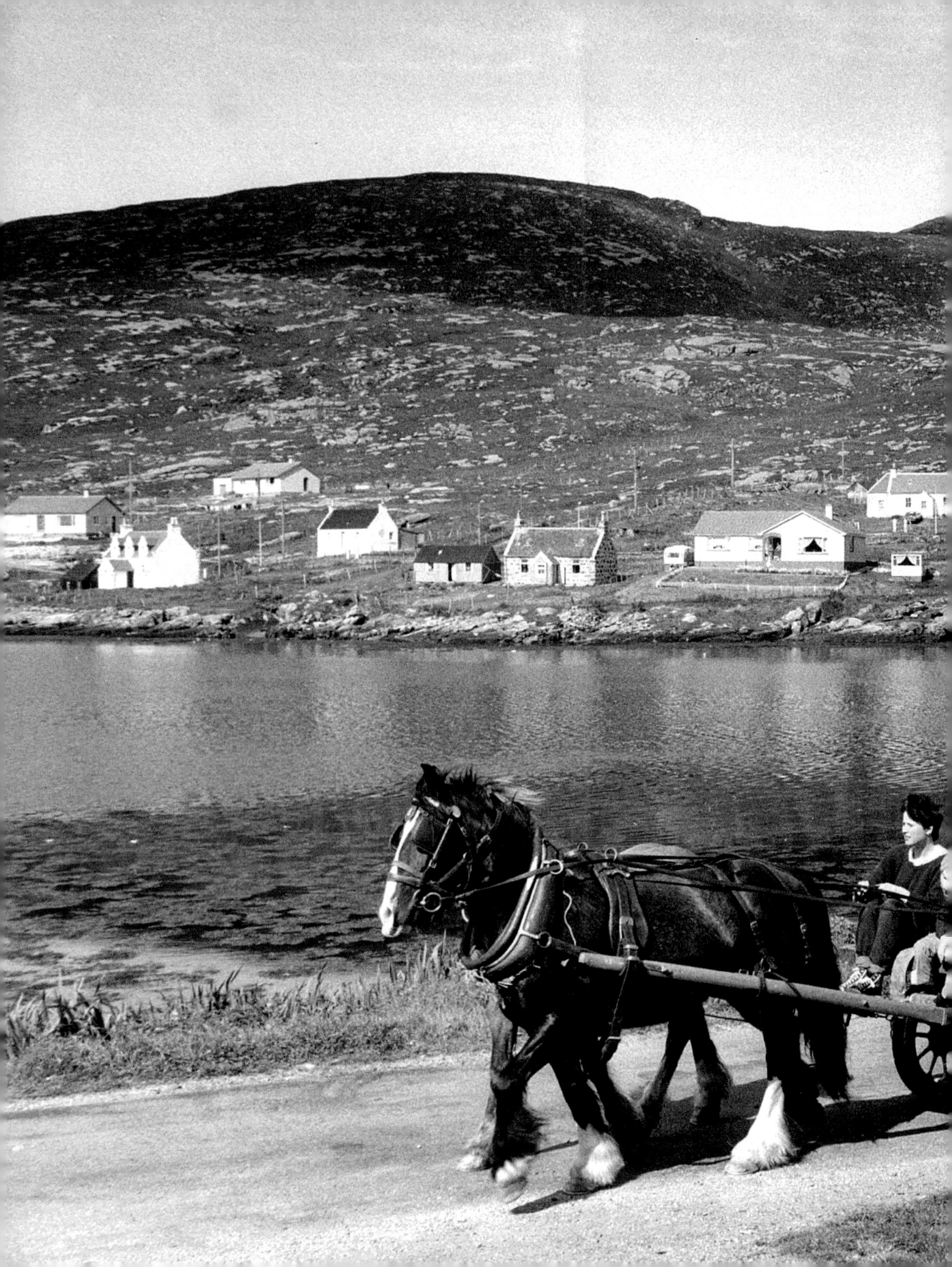

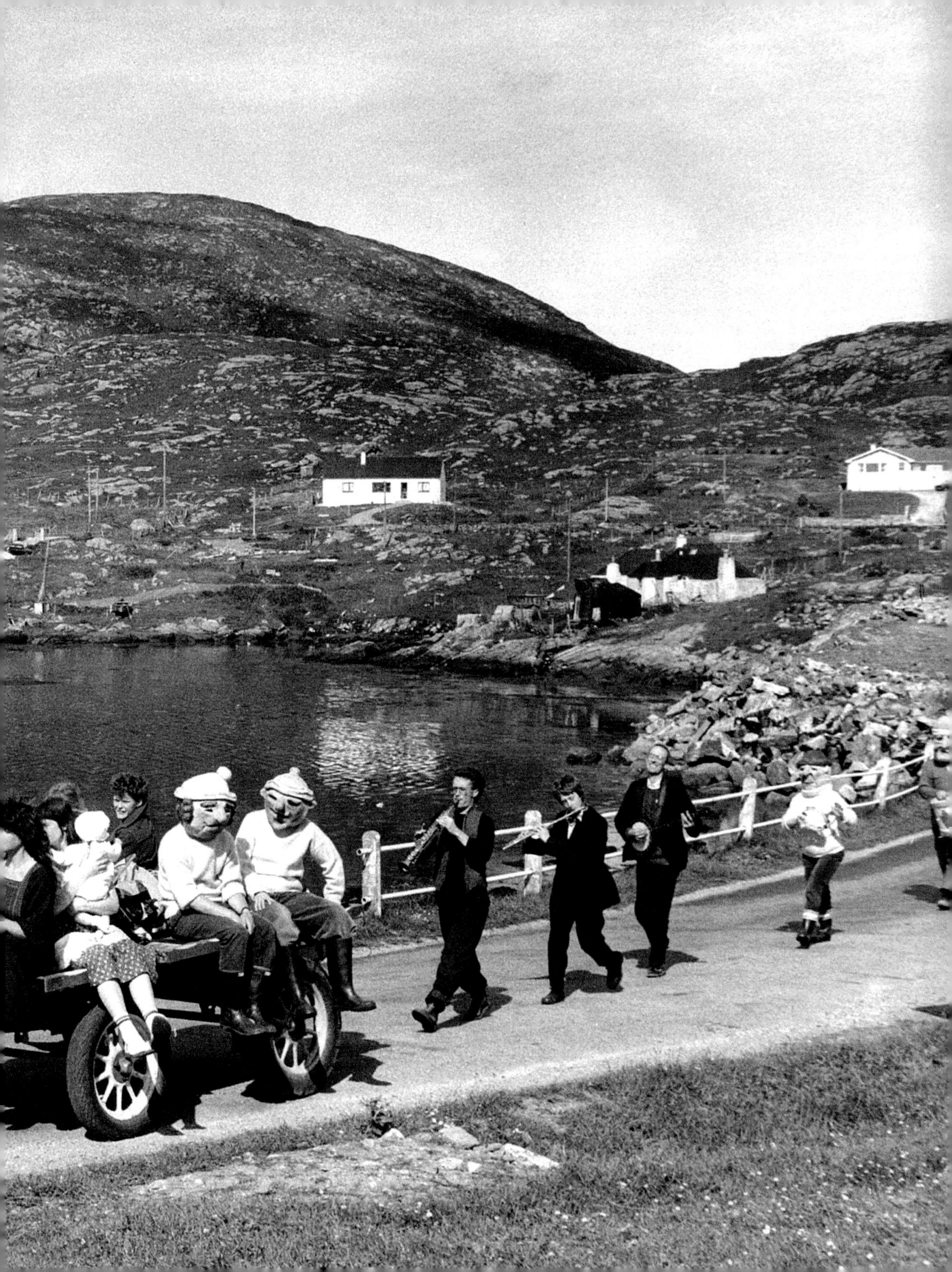

Lewis

I then made my way north, from Eriskay through the Uists and Benbecula, to Berneray and then to Harris. As I went north I moved further away from Catholicism, and by the time I was in North Uist it was clearly a protestant country, a place of the Free Church, the 'Wee Frees'. Early in 1983, with the outline of the tour agreed, I returned with Moira Hirst, our horse-handler, and we plotted out a more precise itinerary for the tour, heading north again, from Vatersay and Barra. At the very end of our journey, in Stornoway, on Lewis, we found that we couldn't work on the Sabbath, as it was strictly frowned on and that even being seen out would have counted against any hope of the company being allowed to visit there. We thought we would just have to stay put and enjoy a quiet Sunday.

We could watch TV and perhaps enjoy the bottle of whisky we kept for emergencies. But late on Saturday the TV was wheeled out of our room. As this was being done, we heard chains clanking outside and, opening the curtain, we saw the swings and roundabouts of the children's playground being locked up so that no child might play on the Sabbath. In the event we decided against Lewis altogether; nothing to do with religion, but the long pull north on the A589 from Harris was daunting and probably not manageable by our horses given the heavy loads they pulled. So our tour had to finish further south, in Tarbert, the largest town of Harris, and nearby Seilobost.

We read the reports of other companies who had made shorter tours of the islands. One result of this was that a friend (Sue MacGovern) went on an advance cycle tour of the route. Sue spoke to locals and put up posters two weeks before our arrival. Mindful of Father Colin's words, I wrote a script based around local themes. A story of a voyage undertaken by a young girl in search of her father and younger brother who had been taken in a storm whilst out fishing. Being wordless it avoided the English versus Gaelic issue, and I was able to weave in a storyline relating to a very topical concern on the islands – the radioactive spill from English nuclear plants such as Windscale, which local fisherman feared threatened the fish stocks.

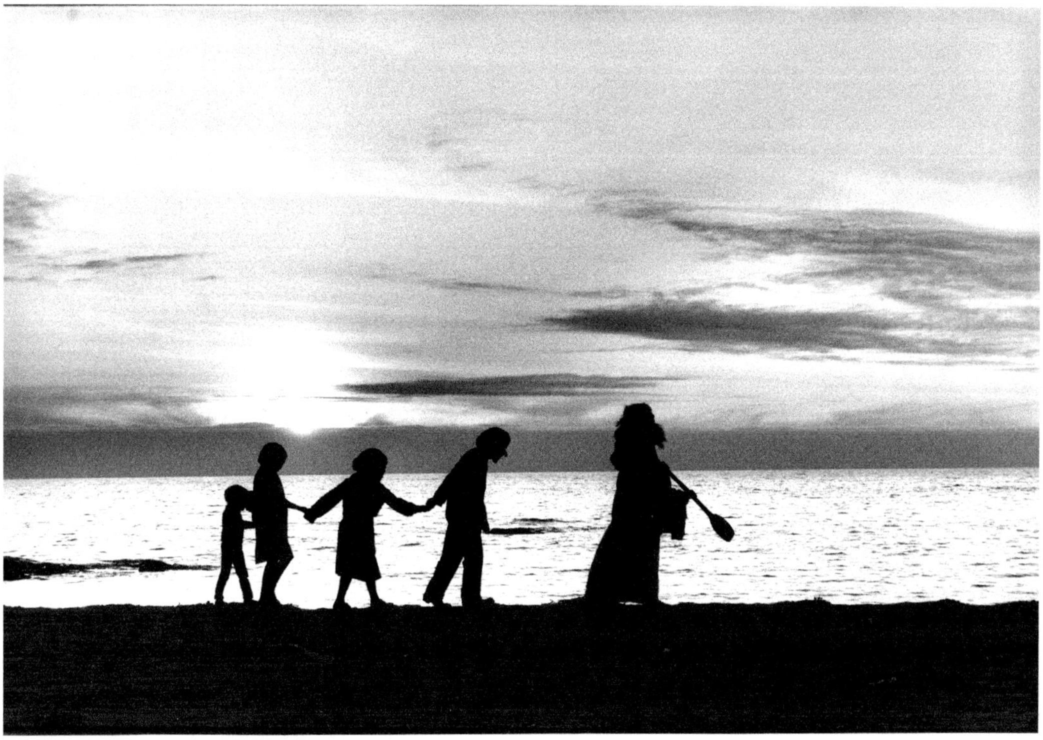

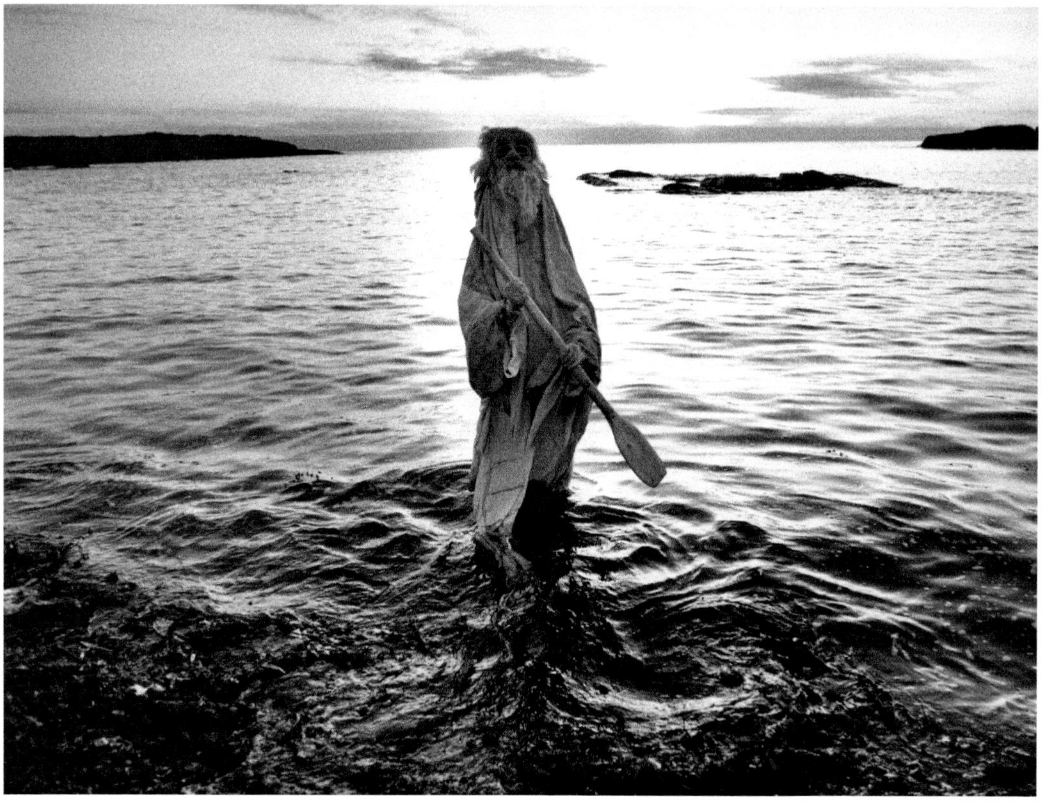

Seòl (pronounced 'shawl') in Gaelic means as a noun 'sail', as a verb 'sail, guide or navigate'. I chose it as the title of the production. In Barra we camped at Tangasdale, a beautiful site near to the friendly Isle of Barra hotel. I wondered if Father Colin would come to see the show. He turned up for our third performance, seemed happy enough, then left after thanking the cast. Next morning we received an invitation to participate in Fèis Bharraigh (Barra Fèis), which opened the next day. The weather was wonderful. Our large parade puppets, including a Kelpie, or Water Horse, led the procession, followed by our band and performers in masks and costumes. Then three trucks carrying local children playing a variety of instruments. That evening we were invited to the local ceilidh in Castlebay, and we joined in with the islanders, enjoying traditional dancing until the early hours of the morning. We were told that we made it seem "like New Orleans (had) come to Barra".

The tour

The tour was memorable to say the least. Two months travelling to 9 islands. Adventures came almost daily. Nowadays there's a causeway to Vatersay, but then it meant a short sea journey. Unfortunately the coal-puffer was docked at the only landing place. So we had to carefully manhandle our equipment – ourselves, musical instruments, parade puppets – over the decks of the puffer before disembarking. Then a mile or so walking to the community for the parade, we passed the almost intact wreckage of a crashed German aircraft left behind from the Second World War. Our report adds "We were suddenly joined by a van load of workmen who were very drunk and very happy. We played for them and talked….they gave us an astonishing display of wrestling."

'The Guardian' flew out arts reporter Robin Thornber and photographer Dennis Thorpe. They stayed with us on Barra for a couple of days, joining in with our lives and reviewing and photographing our work. In the end they felt that Dennis's photographs were so good that they published a full page photo-feature about the tour.

Leaving Barra we travelled to Lochboisdale where we were treated to a spontaneous ceilidh around the campfire – songs, dancing and stories. Then on through South Uist to Eochar (Iochdar) where Angus McPhee had lived, although I only got to know of Angus's story many years later. Then to Carinish, and through North Uist to Lochmaddy and the island of Berneray. On Berneray we arrived on the same day as the Annual Peat Procession and Auction. Like Vatersay there's now a causeway to Berneray but then it also meant a sea journey. Getting the horses onto the deck of a small ferry was now a little easier – we lured them on with carrots. Once there we helped revive the old tradition of using horses and carts to deliver the peat to the crofts dotted around the island. The peat came from the uninhabited island of Torogay, and was loaded onto carts and distributed throughout Berneray. The day ended with a great ceildih and a display of Highland dancing. It went on into the early hours. One of the islanders, Chris Spears, dropped everything and joined us for the rest of the tour. Chris later worked with the company on several occasions, mainly making props for shows. It's through Chris that I one day got to hear the story of Angus McPhee. This led us, thirty years later, to *Angus – Weaver of Grass*, a production in which we properly got to grips with creating theatre for, and with, the Gaelic-speaking communities.

Everywhere that summer the travel days took us through stunning scenery; at every stop we had enthusiastic audiences. The show was well received and one of the most memorable experiences of the company's history. It then went on to a short tour of the north-west of England. This turned out to be the last tour for two years as we spent the summer of 1985 moving into new premises.

64

11. THE MANCHESTER CRIB, 1984

In 1984 I was still lecturing part-time on the Foundation Art course at Manchester Polytechnic. Dean Jowett of Manchester Cathedral had approached the college about creating a new Christmas Crib for the Cathedral. The college suggested that I might want to look at this, and so I went along to the cathedral to meet with the Dean. It turned out that we both shared a passion for the Anglo-Welsh artist David Jones – both his poetry and his visual art work. I was able to persuade the Dean to let me direct a consecration performance in the Cathedral in return for designing and making the crib.

The crib itself consisted of a huge silk canopy with appliqué 'wings' designed by Joan Beadle. These extended into the cathedral's south aisle, and the cloth structure hung over and framed a life-size, carved wooden holy family, positioned inside a tall gauze column that rose up to the cathedral roof.

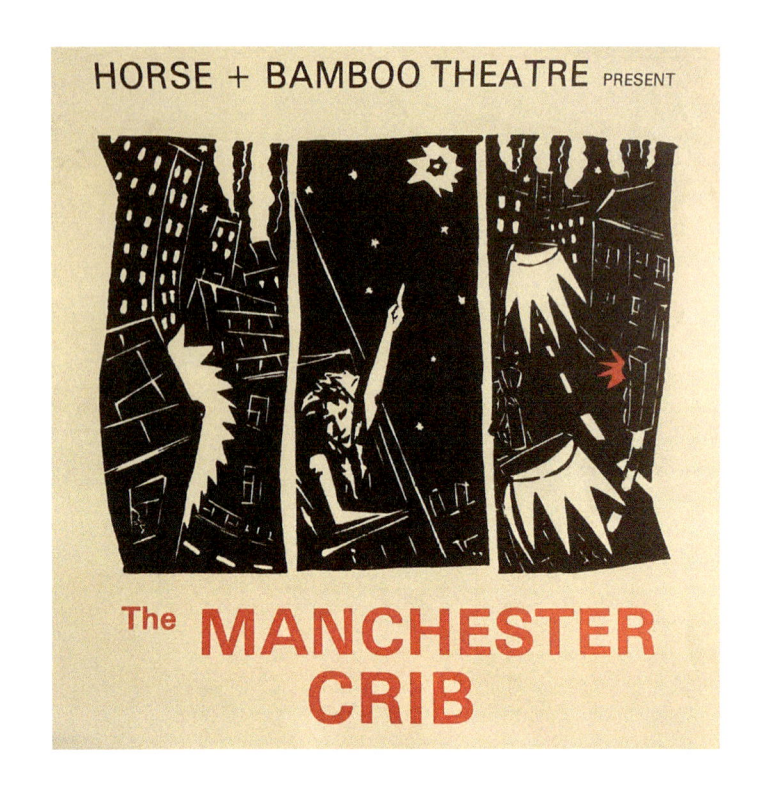

The crib fabric was made by Joan with help from Rona Lee and Liz Mather. The wood and cloth carved figures were designed and made by Don McKinley with Peigi Cole, who did the stitching work with Penny Marrows.

As well as the work of making the crib and surrounds, the consecration performance also involved 16 company members performing the various large-scale puppet and mask parts, assisted by 11 students from the Manchester Polytechnic's Art Foundation Course. The performance was in 7 sections, each with its own visual world, and each separated by a narration. At the climax the cathedral nave and choir were filled with clouds of smoke, and a gigantic rainbow was projected into the aisle, high above the congregation, filling the space.

The largest resources of all were musical, and on the day of the dedication, 23rd December 1984, our composer and Music Director Mick Wilson (who had earlier toured with *Seòl*) oversaw four ensembles – the Athena String Quartet, Gamelan Seka Petak from York, the Tameside Youth Percussion Ensemble and Bramhall High School Gamelan. These were joined by Manchester Cathedral Voluntary Choir and their choirmaster Gordon Stewart on the cathedral organ.

The whole event was through-composed by Mick, including music for the two carols that I wrote to accompany the dedication service. Because of the impossibility of getting the 100 or so performers to rehearse together in advance of the event, everything had to be learned to Mick's precisely timed click-track. Each ensemble then rehearsed their own parts in their own spaces.

The whole event ran perfectly; music, the performances, readings and lighting came together as if by magic; a great tribute to the cast – and Mick's click-track.

Above: Cloth figure of the Virgin and suspended wooden Holy Ghost.
Right: Rona Lee working on the figure of the Virgin Mary.

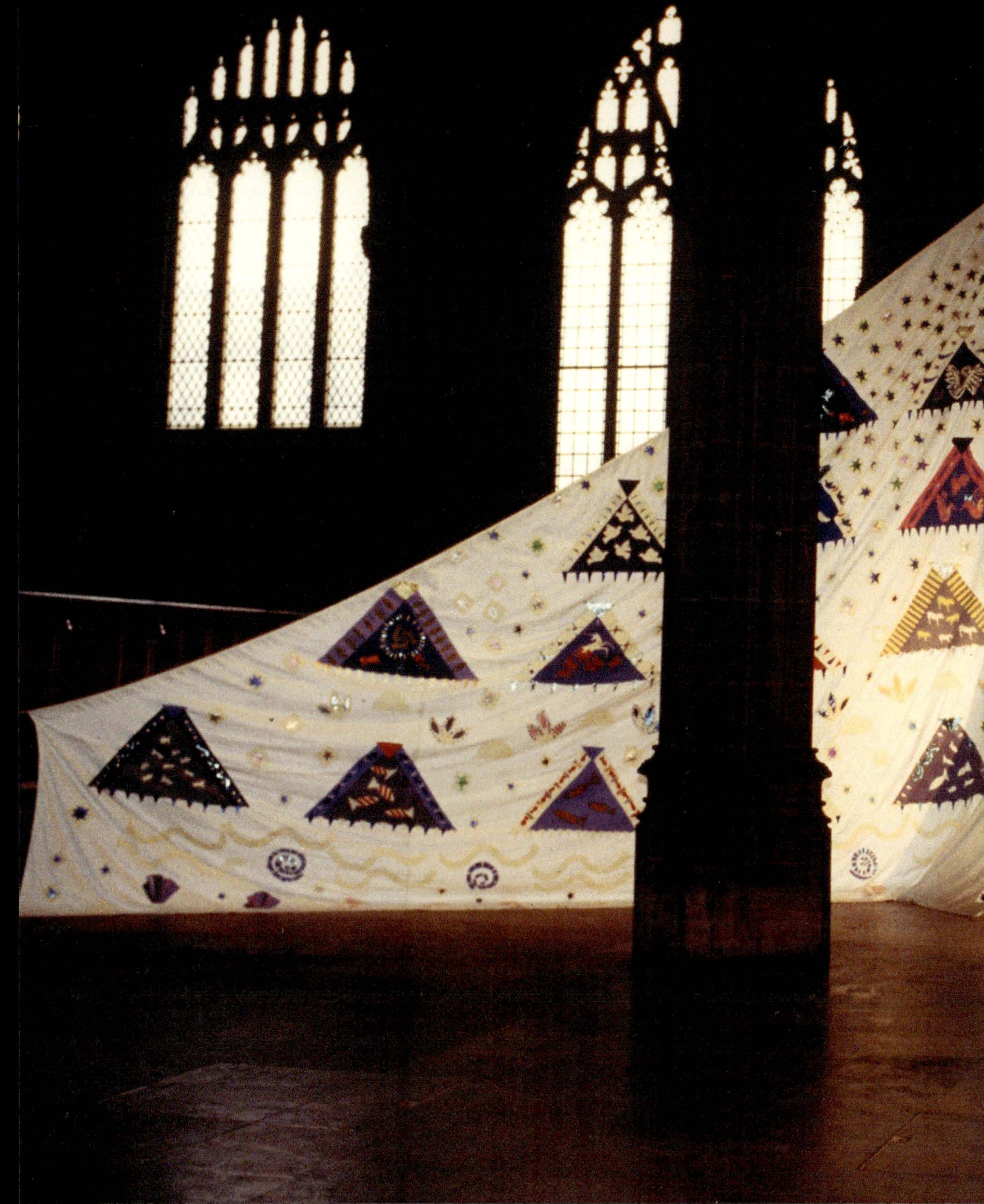

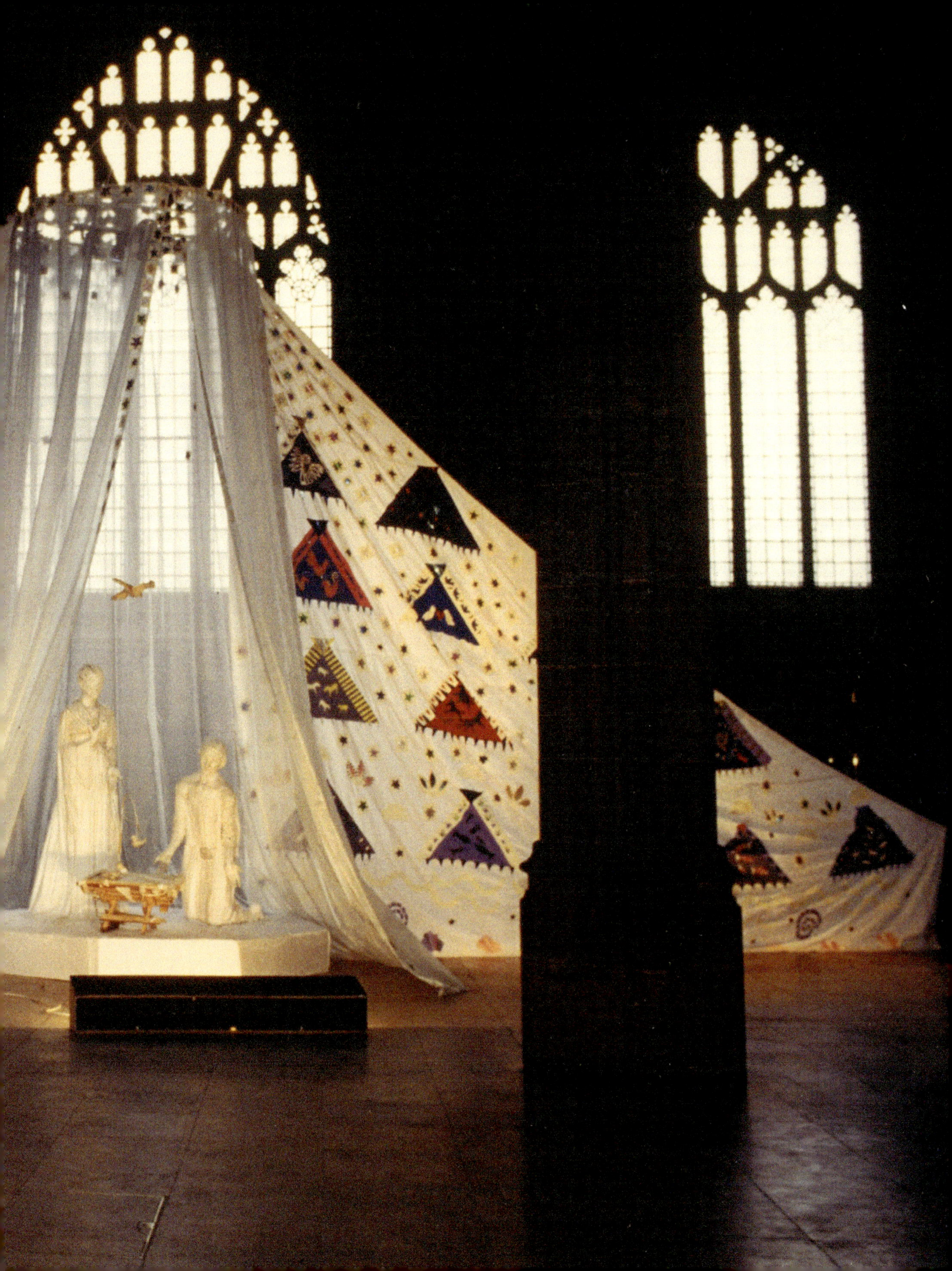

MUSIC

From the beginning live music was an essential part of Horse & Bamboo performances. There was no speech in the shows; it was the music that gave a breath to the performances. Although our early shows were normally accompanied by no more than two or three multi-instrumentalists, the Music Director was always a key member of the team. Then from the mid-1980s the ensembles began to grow in size and ambition. At Manchester Cathedral, Mick Wilson worked with well over 60 musicians. Our community projects would normally put together street bands that were 10 or more strong. Touring shows during the 1990s usually created a street band that involved all of the performers in the show, combining professional and non-professional musicians.

By 2000, improvements in sound technology enabled us to begin to tour with recorded digital music systems in place of live musicians. This change was a gradual one and was made with a heavy heart, and the organic and responsive interchange between the performers, images and music, which was truly intuitive, magical, and would change nightly, slowly faded. This all coincided with a reduction in our Arts Council grant aid, and the urgent need for us to cut costs. Still, music remained at the heart of the theatre performances, and there were undoubtedly certain gains in working to a reliably consistent soundtrack. Enormous efforts continued to go into creating the sound world for each production and, when possible, such as the use of Gaelic song in the *Angus, Weaver of Grass* production, we found ways of continuing to use live music.

This page top: Jo King
Immediately above: Loz Kaye
Right: Yusapha M'boob
Opposite page: Horse & Bamboo at Irwell Day, Rawtenstall

12. TALES FROM A MASKSHOP, 1986

In 1985 the company moved from its very basic workshop in Irwell Vale to much larger premises in Rawtenstall. The new workshop, which had once been a foundry but more recently a garage for a trucking company, required a lot of work, especially cleaning the oily space and adapting it for theatre work. It meant we needed to take the best part of the year out and as a result we didn't re-tour a new production until the following year.

Tales From a Maskshop was based on Kenneth Patchen's disturbing and apocalyptic novel *The Journal of Albion Moonlight*, itself based on the pre-Shakespearian lyric Tom O'Bedlam. It was a huge challenge to adapt this for the stage, so I decided to open with a filmed section, as we had in 1983. A 16 minute, 16mm black and white film, was put together by Steph Bunn and followed the last journey of an old mask maker, filmed in situ in Haslingden and Helmshore. The North West Film Archive have recently digitised the film, and a new sound track has been created by David Chatton Barker and the *Root Folk Band*.

Melissa Wyer acted as narrator, her face masked by a loose veil. In a change to our noramlly wordless theatre I adapted Patchen's words to describe an increasingly wild and surreal journey into an unpromising land, in the aftermath of some unnamed catastrophe.

Initially I decided that the piece would finish with the cast continuing on their bleak journey, stepping off the stage and filing out of the marquee, leaving the audience behind. Thus there would be no curtain call, no possibility of applause or an ending in the normal sense. This divided both our audiences and the cast, and was a genuinely uncomfortable ending, lacking any sense of resolution to the experience of the play. We discussed this over and over among ourselves, and then experimented over the next few performances with different endings. Finally we returned to a more conventional approach, taking a curtain call, and allowing for applause. It was less controversial but I was never totally certain that it had been the right decision.

Then in 1987 we took what seemed like a momentous decision and decided to abandon the marquee and perform in village halls, taking our shows into the community's own spaces. In part this had become inevitable as our large tent took the best part of a day to erect and only made economic sense if we could perform several shows at the site. Promoters who could afford to book us for a run of shows were quickly disappearing as the impact of Mrs Thatcher's cuts to local authority budgets began to take effect. Much of *Tales From a Maskshop*, for a variety of reasons, had been toured using village halls in any case, and it then became our new touring model.

Above image: Still from 16mm film Tales from a Maskshop
Following page: The mask maker in his workshop, still from the film Tales from a Maskshop

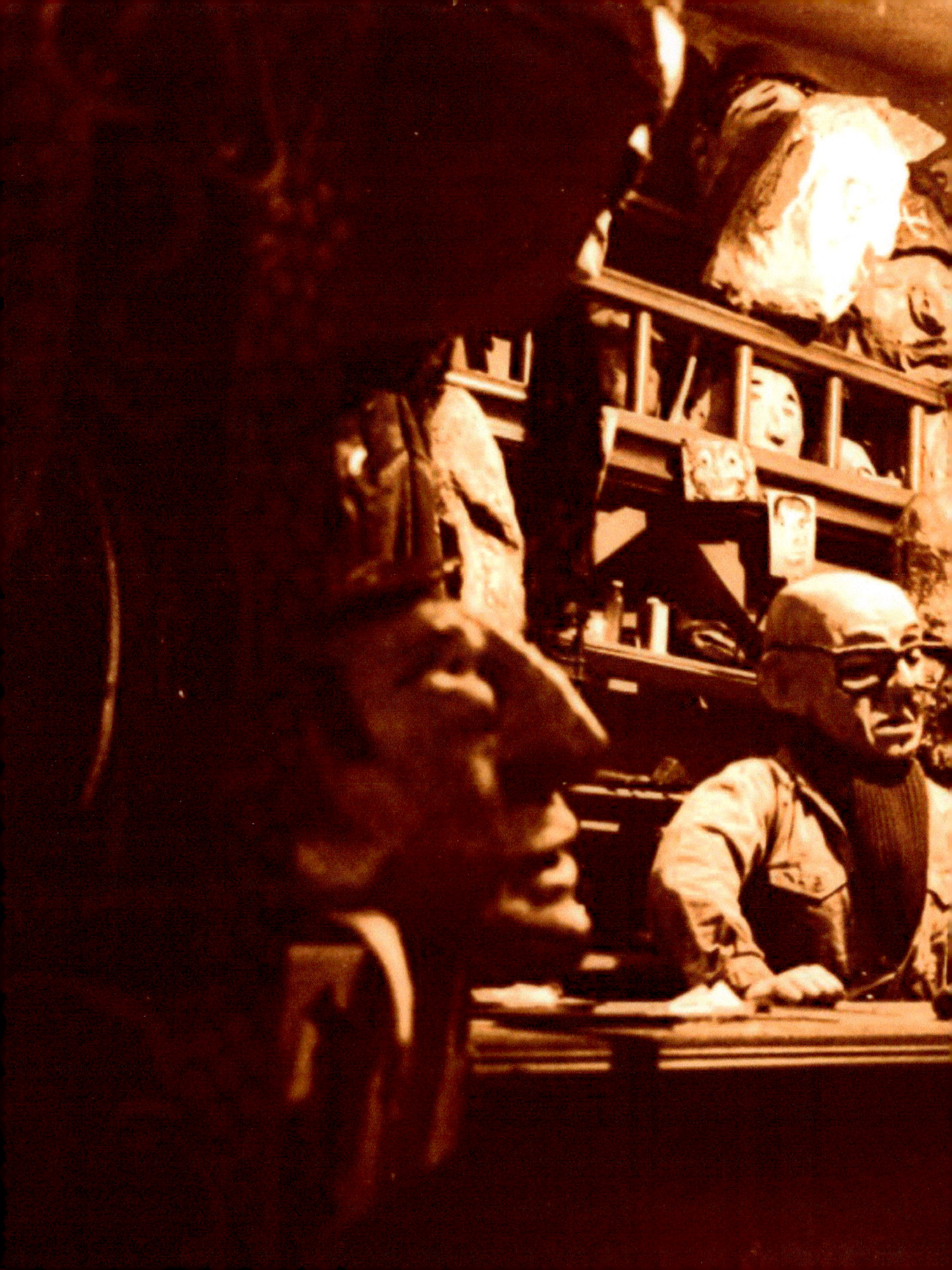

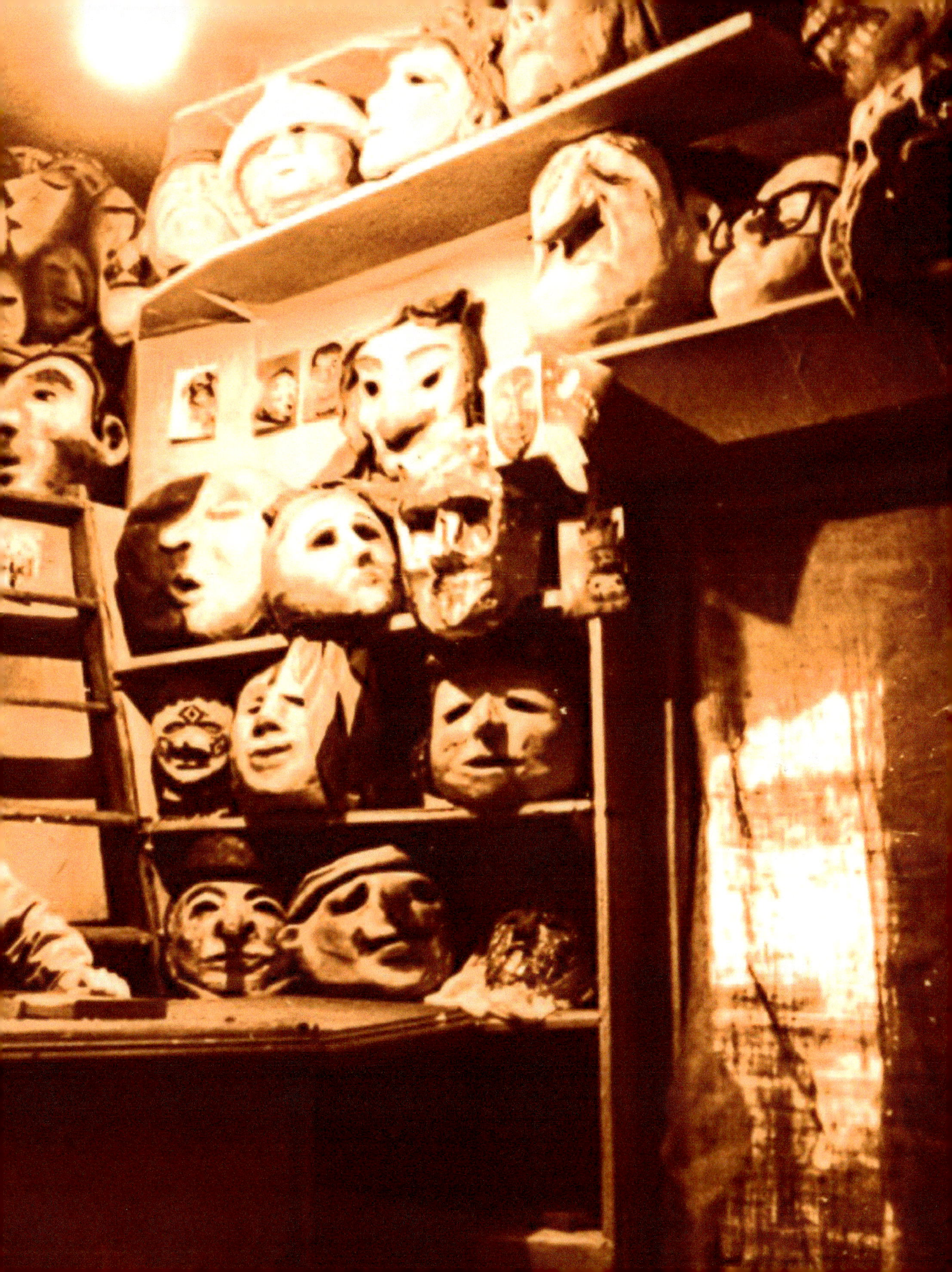

13. THE WHEEL/AN ROTH, 1987/8

In the late 1980s Horse & Bamboo was approaching its tenth anniversary. The horse-drawn tours remained at our centre of gravity, and they had settled into a seasonal cycle, with a new production from late June or July until September. Sometimes we set out from our base, which since 1985 had been in Rawtenstall. But more often than not we packed up horses, wagons and the show into a big horsebox and trailer, and drove to wherever the tour was starting. We also took our van, which carried the technical equipment, the tents and other personal belongings. Once the horse-drawn tour had finished, there would be a short break before we started on a winter programme. The shows during this period tended to have a cast of eight, of whom two or three would be the musicians. At this point we paid every member of the company a flat rate of £145 a week, equivalent to £389 in 2023.

*

In 1987 we were back into a routine, and we were asked by Údarás, the Irish Gaelic language agency for the Gaeltacht, to devise a tour for the West of Ireland. Údarás had heard about our tour of the Outer Islands of Scotland, and suggested something similar. The resulting show was *An Roth*, or *The Wheel*. It was based on a radio-play I had stumbled across years' before, missing the beginning. It was a dark story involving two men who meet a stranger. He promises a handsome reward if they deliver a wheel to another village. They start off, pushing the wheel by hand and thinking it's going to be easy money. They have various quixotic encounters on the way. It's only when they're getting close to their destination, after increasingly strange confrontations, that the truth dawns on them – that the wheel is going to be used to break the body of a prisoner. It reminded me of the image of wheels on skeletal poles in the background of Brueghel's painting 'The Triumph of Death'.

We still have the tour diary for 1987 – it's a reminder of how complicated touring abroad was in pre-EU days. It involved carnets, and ours had an attached list of 250 numbered items that had to be described in full ('one detachable tin puppet nose') and then sealed to await customs inspection. At the Port of Dublin we were nearly sent back home because there were a few strands of loose hay on the floor of the horse box. Now these joys have once again returned, thanks to Brexit.

But having weathered that potential catastrophe we literally walked into a series of others. On Thursday 9th July we arrived in Dingle to find that the drays had arrived a day earlier than planned. They had been roughly dumped by the carrier, Pandoro, at our planned campsite, and had been damaged. On Saturday 11 July we opened with our first show – the diary says 'from the beginning… things seemed to go well. People's eyes were caught by the magic of it. They laughed at all the right moments and gasped at the tense ones. At the end we were asked back for two curtain calls. People crowded round to tell us how much they enjoyed it…'. R.T.E asked us if they could broadcast the whole tour on national radio.

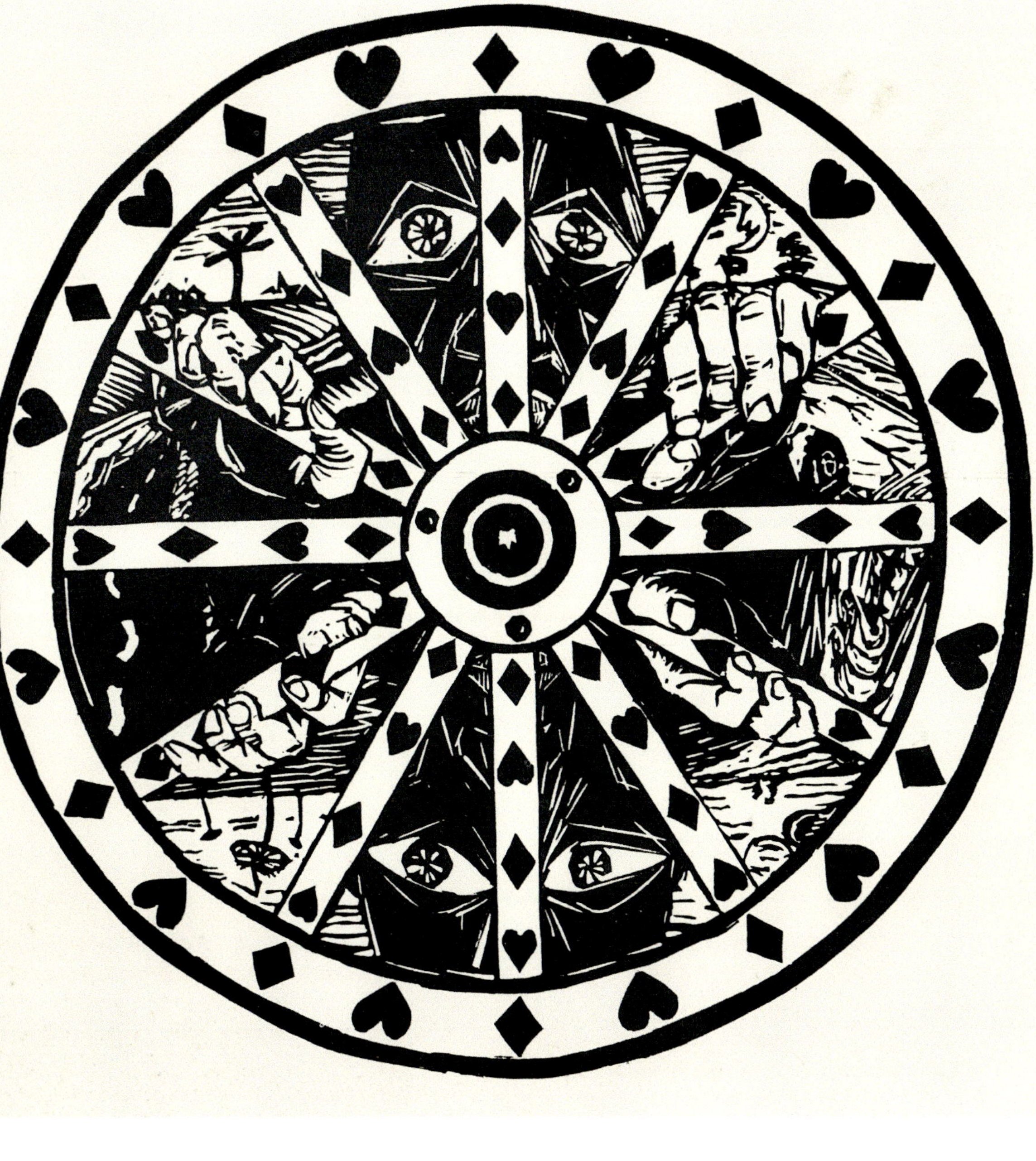

An injury

That night we sat round the fire full of good humour, feeling encouraged and confident that it would be a successful tour. Then disaster happened – Steph Bunn left the fireside to go behind a bush and stumbled in the dark, damaging her foot. In the morning we took her to the medical centre, and we were told that she had badly torn a ligament. Her leg was put in plaster. Luckily our administrator, Sue Williams, was with us for the beginning of the tour and she gamely stepped into Steph's role. The next day, the Sunday performance, was attended by a representative of the British Council.

The damaged drays had to be repaired and we urgently needed to work out how to deal with Steph's injury. Meanwhile we were about to embark on a horse-drawn tour of one of the remotest parts of Ireland. Steph couldn't walk, but at first she was told that her plaster could come off in two weeks. But when we reached that deadline another hospital visit advised that this would actually need to be eight weeks. Sue couldn't stay with us for that long, and so we had to ask Jill Swales, the student who had been doing lighting for us, if she would swap roles with Steph.

We didn't need to cancel any shows, and the performances were reasonable. But we all knew that we were only just getting by, and it wasn't improving in the way that we would normally expect it to as the show bedded in. Having to grab short periods for rehearsal, and frequent trips to clinics with Steph took up all of our spare time. 'Owing to the accident we were simply treading water...' says one entry in the tour diary. Inevitably the incident left Steph feeling extremely dejected too.

Then at the end of July, Jill injured her back and she too was in a lot of pain. Kay Kennedy happened to be visiting and she volunteered to stand in for Jill. But Kay couldn't stay with us for the duration of the tour, and we decided that there was nothing for it but to fly a permanent replacement out from England. The whole experience was an illustration as to how fragile life on the road could be. In fact we were generally very fortunate, and in over 20 years of horse-drawn touring these turned out to be the most serious mishaps we encountered by far. We managed well, at least in the sense that the tour went ahead without cancellations. Other years we had injuries, but either we were closer to home and able to substitute performers more easily, or the injuries healed themselves within a day or two. In 1987 however, there was no doubt that this string of unfortunate events affected the quality of the production.

The Island – Inis Bofin

The tour of 1987 included a short residency on the island of Inis Bofin (The Island of the White Cow) in early September. The weather had broken and the crossing was delayed by storms, though we finally sailed on Paddy's mailboat, 'The Glorious', on the 5th September despite warnings from some of the locals that it was too dangerous (the diary quotes overhearing one saying it was a 'suicide mission'). I let the team make their own decisions, and Tim Petter chose to remain behind on the mainland that evening. This was possible since we weren't performing the show, but were putting together a parade and a fire sculpture in the harbour. The mailboat was heavily laden and crammed with goods, and we had to hunker down under tarpaulins to protect us from the high seas. It was indeed a heart-in-mouth crossing, especially as the boat had been out once earlier in the day but turned back because of engine trouble. Gannets skimmed across the rough waves and most of us were soaked through. One young boy, the diary tells us, was sick over Tim Bender's trousers. However the weather rapidly improved, the next day was glorious, and with Tim Petter back the group reunited.

In 1988 we revived *An Roth*, now with its English title *The Wheel*, for a tour of North East England (including 2 nights on Holy Island), Dumfries & Galloway and the Scottish Borders.

REVIEW:

"….The Wheel is a mixture of myth, music, mime, legend and symbolism depicting the trials and the triumphs of an elderly couple along life's way. And that's as far as I can get to setting the scene for you. Almost every art form you can think of, with the exception of the spoken word, is brought into play and if you think this sounds like eclecticism run riot let me assure you it is not. The actors wears full-head masks, human and animal, in a succession of scenes which are by turn exciting, comic and chilling. A pair of stags lock antlers in combat, a man is broken on the wheel after an encounter with a sinister, monkish figure.

"The relevance of one scene to another, and the interpretation of each scene is left to the audience so this is not a play for the literal-minded. But to the uncluttered imagination of children it presents no problem.

"It was like a dream, with its fleeting images alternately nightmarish and serene and always inconsequential, born of experiences on the west coast of Ireland…The musicians, performers, lighting technicians and other members of this amazing company have provided us with an unforgettable theatrical experience."

Richard Kelly, The Guardian, 12 July 1988

14. PILTON RESIDENCY, 1987

The Beaford Centre, now Beaford Arts, was established by Dartington Hall Trust, and at the time was Europe's largest rural arts centre. At the beginning of 1986 the company was asked by Beaford's Rick Bond to consider a residency based at Pilton. Not the Glastonbury one, but Pilton on the outskirts of Barnstaple in Devon. The idea was to work towards a large-scale event at Easter 1987, far bigger than other community-based events we had undertaken, it would also celebrate the 21st anniversary of the Beaford Centre itself. A small group of us would live in the village from February, gradually being joined by others until 17 Horse & Bamboo artists would be working with the village community to create events in late April.

I met with Rick and we visited Pilton, where we were introduced to some of the people from the community and explored the village. In September a group from Horse + Bamboo paid a second visit; then in December 1986 I went to Pilton with Sue Goodwin from Rakuworks, which operated as a kind of sister company to Horse & Bamboo. It had been set up by Sue and Laura Barnes, both ex-students of mine. Rakuworks specialised in community ceramics events, often around dramatic kiln firings, and we mounted an exhibition about the work of both companies.

We also continued our research into the village and its history, and began to make further contacts with interested local people and groups. Pilton is a fascinating place, with an unusual number of odd features; very much the quintessential English village, with a medieval church with leper squints, a Green Man, and even its own priory. It also had a history of 'pageants' involving the community; a Lady Well; a standing stone and no end of quirky corners and unusual traditions. I began to feel that a celebration of all of these things should be at the heart of the project, and I came up with the idea of 12 curlicues of Pilton. A curlicue being the knot of hair once favoured by sailors, like a small curly pigtail.

On the 9th February 1987 I was joined in Pilton by Steph Bunn and Robin Morley, and the three of us based ourselves in a terraced house in the heart of the village. We followed up on the initial contacts, sourced materials and established 33 community groups who were going to work with us. Mary Plumb soon joined to direct and lead the music. By the 16th March there were 11 members of the company living and working in the village, and shortly afterwards Sue and Laura from Rakuworks arrived to work with community groups to make a permanent mosaic village sign. 18 groups met regularly to create the 'curlicues' (sideshows) or to help with creating parades and processions. Other groups worked with Mary to create a village band and worked on a specially commissioned piece of music.

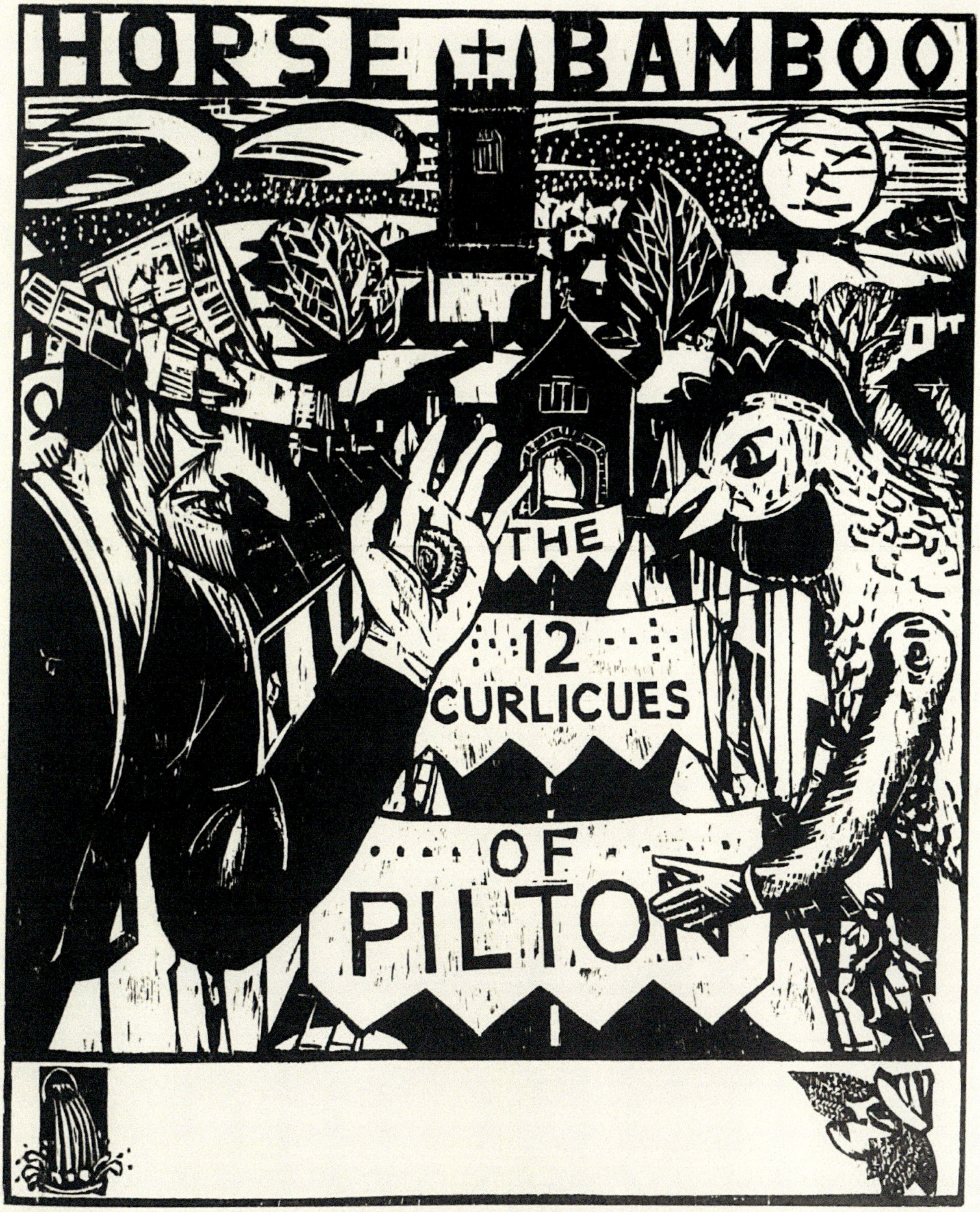
HORSE + BAMBOO
THE
12
CURLICUES
OF
PILTON

Above: The snail mask, worn by Rona Lee to lead the Green Man Parade

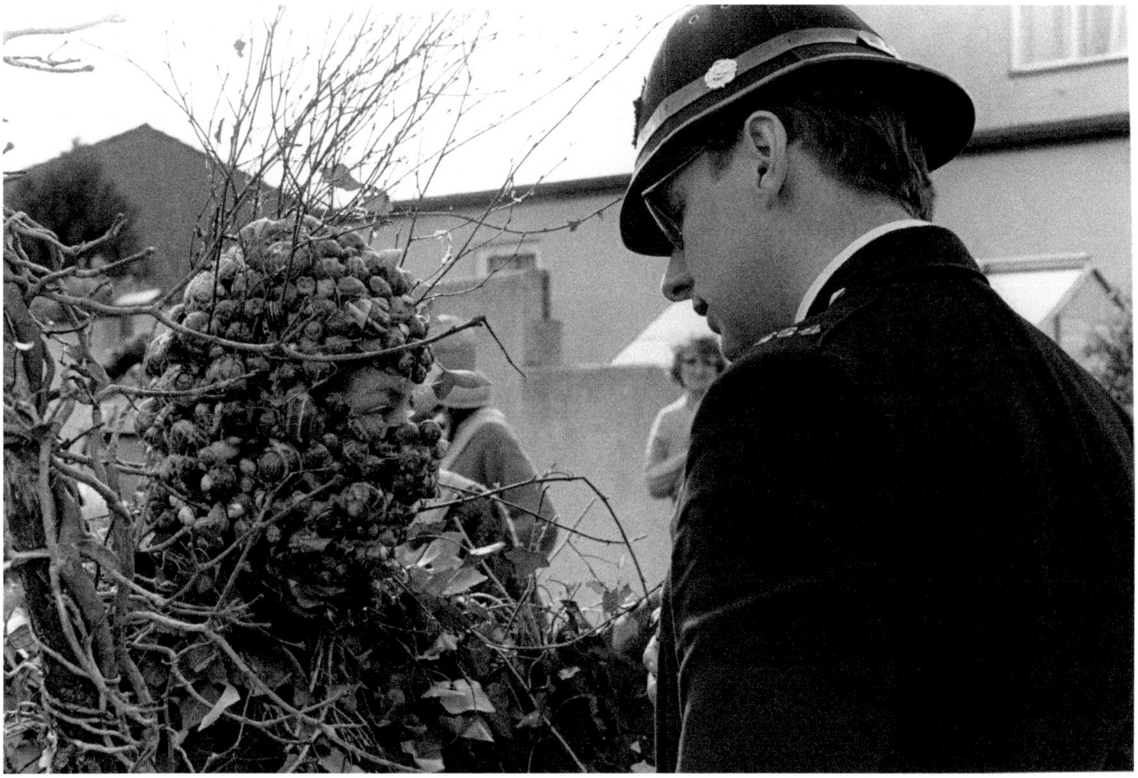

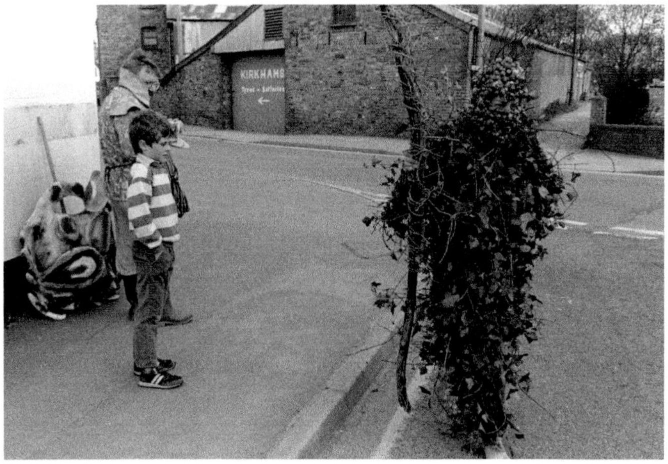
KIRKHAMS

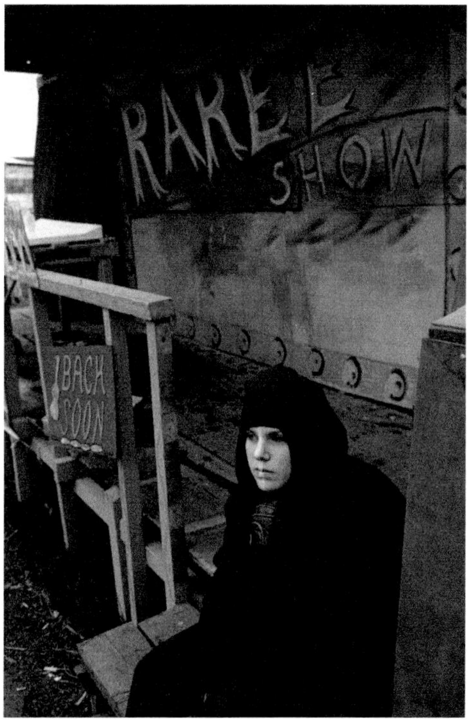
RAREE
SHOW
BACK
SOON

The events culminated over Easter. There were three processions, one each day – a Good Friday Lantern Procession; an Easter Sunday Bell Procession, and an Easter Monday Carnival Procession. The local park, sitting in the meander of the River Yeo, was commandeered for a fairground, with every stall and event hand-made and overseen by Bernard Tindall, with lots of help from the community. There was also a grand final event, the Raising of the Green Man. All of this was communicated to the villagers in the 'Curlicue Times' news-sheet that was overseen by Robin. In all there were three editions, with every household in the village receiving one. In the first edition local people chose which of the many features of their village should make up the twelve 'curlicues'.

Roughly 500 people were directly involved in creating the events. There were many local stalls in the park, as well as a bandstand, a maze, a menagerie made by Steph with local students, a cafe, mystery passages, tree-planting, a story-telling centre, a cinema, a shadow show and a central performance area. The whole event was recorded by the village in an illustrated book 'The Curlicue Scrapbook', which celebrated *The 12 Curlicues* with photographs, reproductions from my notebooks and the 'Curlicue Times', along with comments and memories from many of the villagers

Immediatley above: Robin Morley in Pilton Park

15. THE PLAITED PATH, 1989

The Plaited Path was my version of 'Rapunzel', and it turned out to be a popular show with audiences. I performed in it as a kind of Master of Ceremonies, and this change had the benefit of enabling me to direct most of the show from out front. In previous shows I had been a performer, but then I saw Tadeuz Kantor with his Polish company at the Riverside studio in London. Kantor didn't so much perform in the piece, as haunt it. He popped in and out, shuffling around, tweaking the performers costumes, and even occasionally peeking from behind the curtain to check on us, the audience. I loved all of this, I couldn't put my finger on why exactly, but it sure enhanced things.

With previous shows we had brought in an outside director for the final week or so of rehearsals. I was becoming increasingly bothered with this situation, feeling that despite everyones' best efforts the shows still didn't quite turn out the way I wanted. Sometimes I worked with the musicians, cueing and playing percussion, but I still couldn't 'see' the show properly from that position. *Plaited Path* definitely benefited from me having an outside eye on the production, and it further increased my confidence as a director. Rehearsal periods, which in the earlier shows were frequently measured in days, now had weeks put aside for them, alongside the start of a new sense of discipline and rigour.

The staging, made by Tim Bender, was divided into three areas. In the centre was the tower of the Witch's Castle. Stage left there was a space representing Rapunzel's cell. Balancing this, stage right, I shared a space with the musicians, Mary Plumb and Lisa Otter-Barry. Anne Barber played the Rapunzel role, Adam Strickson was a comedy Witch, with Tim as her bumbling son. These last two characters were based on an aged restaurateur and her son who waited on Kay and myself at a bizarre traditional restaurant in Toledo, Extremadura, in central Spain in which the only item on the menu were huge plates of lamb, piled high in menacing heaps of smashed bones and dark meat.

*

Shortly after this tour I decided to stop performing altogether and concentrate fully on writing, making and directing. This was finally accompanied by my recognition of something that I suspect everyone else had known for several years - that we were now a theatre company, rather than an eccentric branch of the visual arts. Until the mid 1980s I still thought of myself as essentially a visual artist, and the fact that Horse & Bamboo was funded by North West Arts Association as a Visual Arts rather than a Drama company, helped sustain that illusion. But about this time we were moved across to the Drama panel, and slightly grudgingly I finally accepted that I had become, in fact, a theatre director. In this I was encouraged by some of the new people joining the company, particularly Tim Bender, who had come from a theatre background, and who felt strongly that the company (and I) would benefit from absorbing some theatre disciplines, such as introducing group warm-up and focus sessions before shows and rehearsals.

HORSE + BAMBOO THEATRE PRESENT

THE PLAITED PATH

Horse-drawn Summer Tour 1989

HORSE-DRAWN THEATRE

(NOTE: NOT SUITABLE FOR UNACCOMPANIED CHILDREN)

Images from The Plaited Path

16. THE WISH, 1990

Anne Barber had joined Horse & Bamboo in 1986 and became Assistant Director shortly afterwards. Anne who, like Jo King, had studied theatre at Dartington, immediately began to contribute a lot to the company. Her vitality and drive kept us going at a period when we had just moved to new, considerably larger premises. But in 1990 Anne left to spend the best part of a year on sabbatical with *Bread & Puppet Theatre* in Vermont. It meant that the 1990 touring show, *The Wish*, was without her for the first time in several years.

The Wish was yet another edgy story, with a political subtext which had elements in common with the radical street theatre scene of the period. It was inspired by an Indian art movie that I had seen, which opens with a young married woman making an offering at a shrine. She is childless and praying that the gods will bless her with a child. Her husband is a mute, and seen by the village gangsters as a fool and incompetent, and most probably impotent. Of course his lack of speech was impossible to convey in our speechless theatre.

In my version the shrine happens to be right next to the village well, where water is hand-drawn using a bucket on a rope. The villagers are having constant failures of their water supply and so are frequently threatened with drought, which naturally panics everyone. Then a stranger arrives, full of slippery charm, and convinces the villagers that he can build a smart pump mechanism that will solve their water problems. He does this, and they herald him as a saviour, lavishing favours on him. However, before long, he begins to charge for access to the water. A scale of charges is attached to the well and through this he gains control over the village. The young woman we saw at the opening of the story decides to confront him. He tries to seduce her, and when he fails he pulls out a knife and drags her onto the ground...

Sarah Frangleton in the lead role and Jo King as the villainous Stranger, with a largely new team of performers, rose to the challenge of this complex and difficult story. The touring set included a masterclass of onstage plumbing created by Tim Bender, who created a working on-stage water-well that transformed from a bucket to a system of taps. This contraption of pipes and pumps had to be fitted to the well as part of the action of the play. It was then used to pump water into various bottles and buckets as necessary.

This was the production we took to Northern Ireland. The Northern Irish Arts Council had heard of our tours in the Republic, and they asked me to consider a tour of the North. This was during the Troubles, and it seemed important to take an in-depth look at what such a tour would mean for the company. This led me to undertake a sometimes scary reconnaissance of the Border areas. This I did on my own, and I got into so many scrapes zig-zagging between the Republic and the North. As a result I decided that touring the Borders would be too stressful, particularly for our horses. Military helicopters suddenly rising from a small woodland and buzzing a few deafening yards overhead; army patrols emerging from roadside ditches; midnight visits to the campsite. These were things that would have spooked the calmest of horses, let alone performers.

We did eventually tour in Northern Ireland, including much of the lovely Antrim coast. Here we were made welcome both in Orange and Catholic communities. Orangemen were especially drawn to horses, which led to a few bizarre and slightly unsettling encounters.

Motorised touring

The Wish was also the first show we tried as part of a motorised tour. It involved buying a large truck which would work as a sleeping space for the cast. It was nicely painted with a huge half-human, half-horse head on the sides. The plan was helped by working with Gary Hill as our technician and Mafalda da Camara as a performer. Gary and Maf came with their young son Manny and their own Mercedes live-in van.

At the end of the summer tour Anne Barber returned from her sabbatical year with *Bread & Puppet Theatre* in Vermont. Unexpectedly Anne brought along Brad Harley, who had been a *Bread & Puppet* performer and maker, and Brad asked if he, in turn, could now have a sabbatical period with us at Horse & Bamboo. Brad slipped easily into a new role on our motorised tour, and was always fun to have around. Anne and Brad later married and a few years later they went to live on Ward's Island, off Toronto, where they set up their own *Shadowland Theatre*.

The motorised touring experiment didn't survive that first year. The on-board accommodation turned out to be far too cold and uncomfortable in all sorts of ways. On top of that the new truck was slow and cumbersome, especially when navigating narrow country lanes – and it just happened that much of the tour took place in Cornwall. A bad mistake.

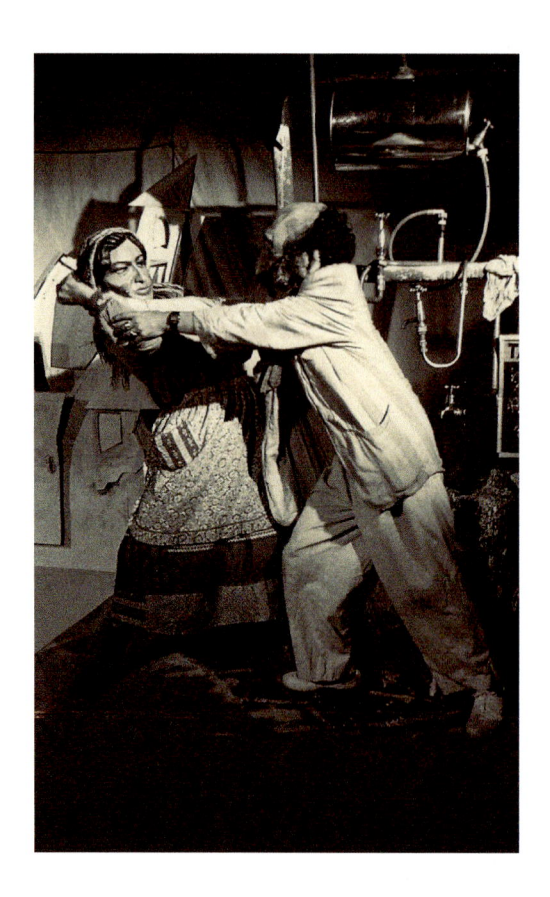

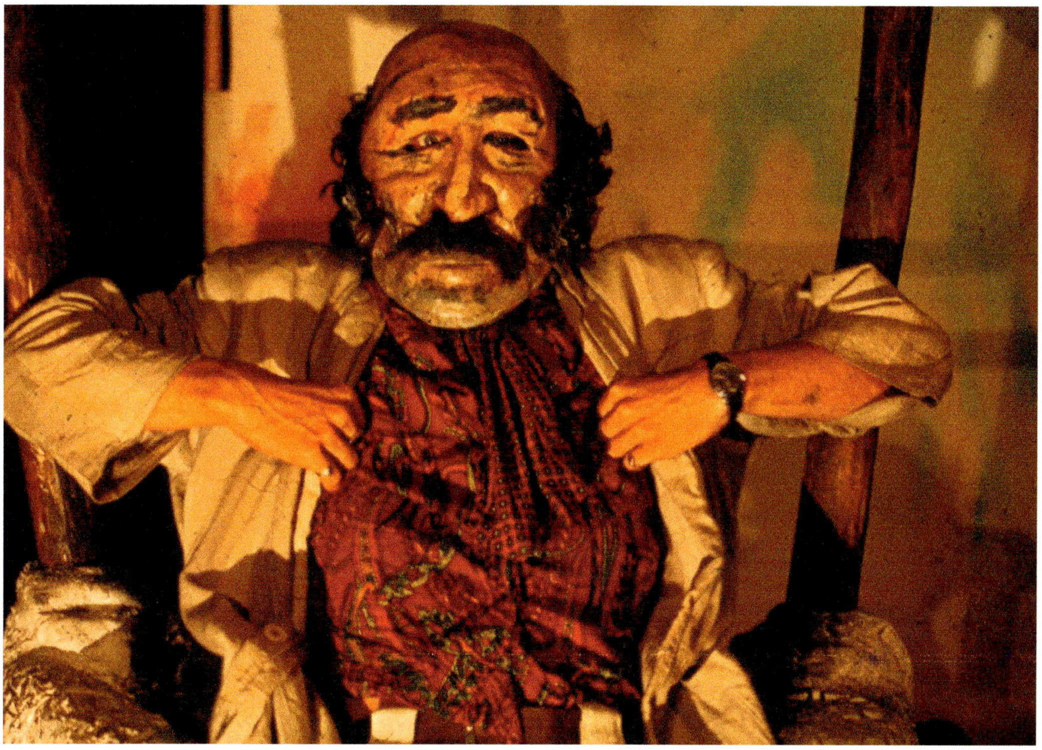

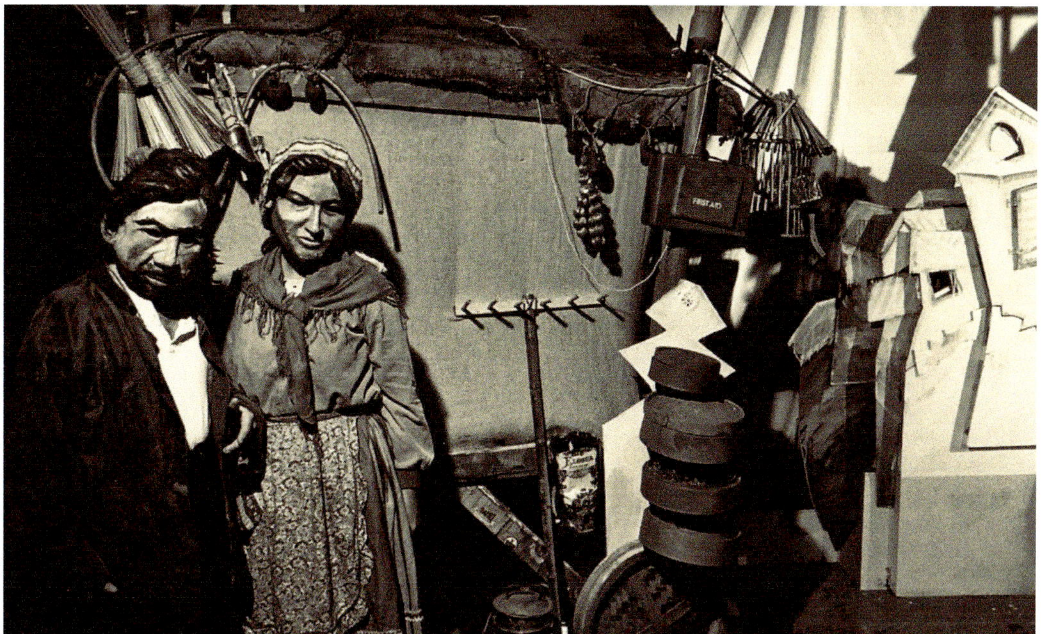

MASKS

Masks were the most distinctive feature of our theatre, and were the key to its visual and wordless form. We nearly always used full-head masks in our productions, which of course meant that speaking was next to impossible for the performers. I made the majority of these, although other company members did contribute. When Alison Duddle joined the company she began to share the mask-making with me. It was probably the job I enjoyed most, creating a character, a life, from clay.

JG Passada from A Strange & Unexpected Event, 1982

Masks from The Moon Watcher, 2018

92

Masks by Alison Duddle, for Veil, 2008

Above Right: Masks from Beyond the Boundary, a project about the Lancashire Cricket League
Above left: Showing them as part of Rossendale Carnival, Bacup, 1998

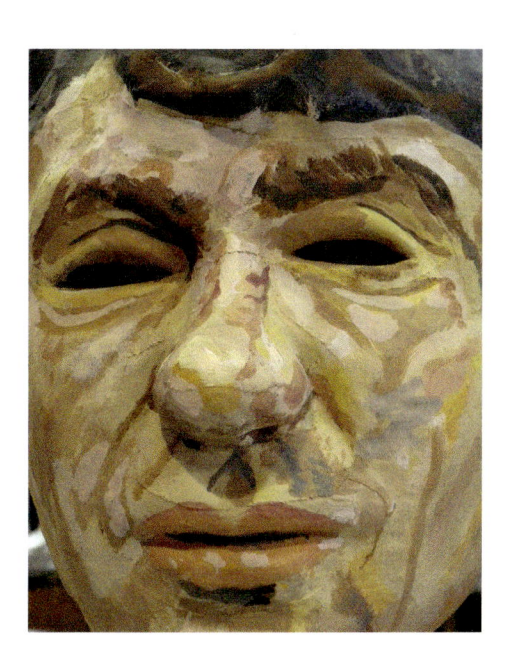

Immediately above left: Mask from Angus, Weaver of Grass, 2012
Right: Close-up of mask of young Angus showing paint detail

94

17. THE FLOOD, 1991

The Flood was the first show in which I didn't perform at all, which meant I was able to direct without distractions. Of course it also meant that I didn't need to tour with the company either, something I felt ambivalent about, since I had grown to love the life on the road, especially walking and working with the horses. Still, I got to visit the company frequently, and was able to give my notes to the company at those times.

I decided on a poetic and disjointed story-line, based loosely on bible stories. It was an odd show; one of my personal favourites. There were four scenes. In the first, the Warning, a sleepy Carpenter is warned of a forthcoming deluge by a stove-pipe hatted delegation. They try and explain the seriousness of the situation. But he refuses to listen to the warnings, and he returns back to bed. In the second, the Search, the Carpenter sees that the prediction had been correct. He witnesses a terrible deluge, and the members of the delegation all drown in front of his eyes. He builds a boat to see if he can find a way to stop the interminable downpour. After an epic voyage he finds the giant figure of Rain, living in a forest.

In the third scene, animals appear out of the forest, fleeing from the rising waters, and creep into his boat. He ends up with a Noah's Ark-like cargo. The animals squabble, then begin to fight, and this sinks the boat. Finally, in The Story of Hope, or The Rumour, crowds of figures appear, seeming to move at random. Then a small crib-like boat appears, holding a new-born baby. The crowd of figures gradually began to move together. They look one way, and then the other. Finally they gently blow and sway together... their breath slowly blowing the child to safety.

Anne had now left for Canada with Brad. Jo King, played the character of the Carpenter. Jo was an amazingly skilled performer, as well as a gifted musician. He was a key member of the company for many years. The music for this show, by John Moreton and Keith Bray was also particularly memorable.

Another important decision we took at this time was to integrate our tours. Once the summer horse-drawn tour ended we continued to tour the same show, but now using our van. The abortive experiment with the truck as part of *The Wish* tour was a precursor to this. But in abandoning the attempt at sleeping in vehicles, the Travelodge necessarily became our friend. In the case of *The Flood* it meant the tour could continue until the end of November, and play as many as 60 venues. The motorised tour of The Flood involved a further 34 performances once the horses had been put back in their field. This routine then became the new norm for the company.

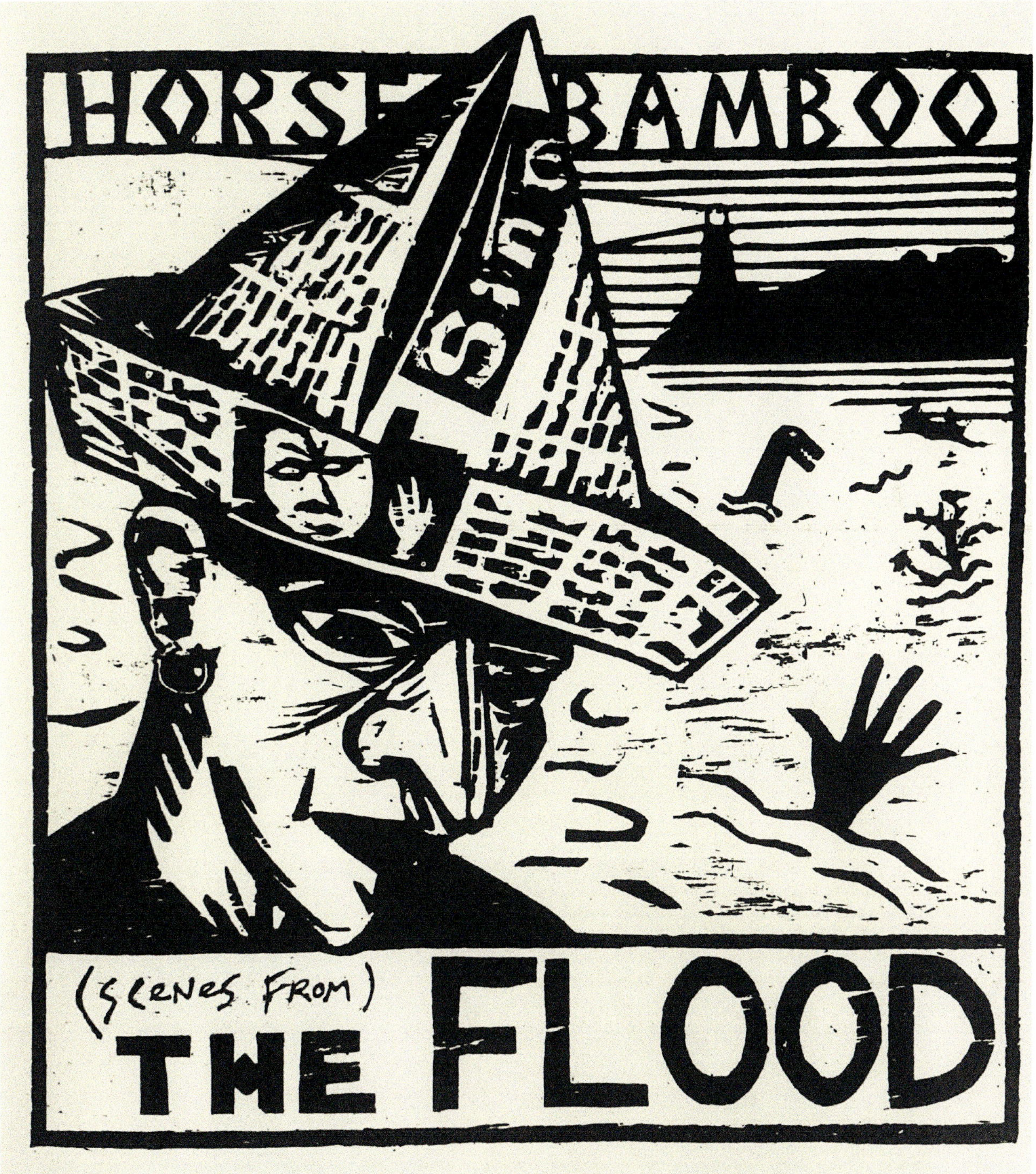
HORSE BAMBOO
(SCENES FROM) THE FLOOD

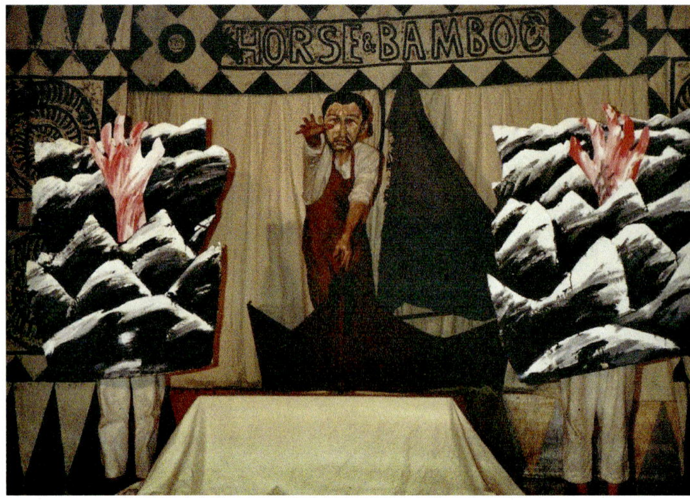
HORSE&BAMBOO

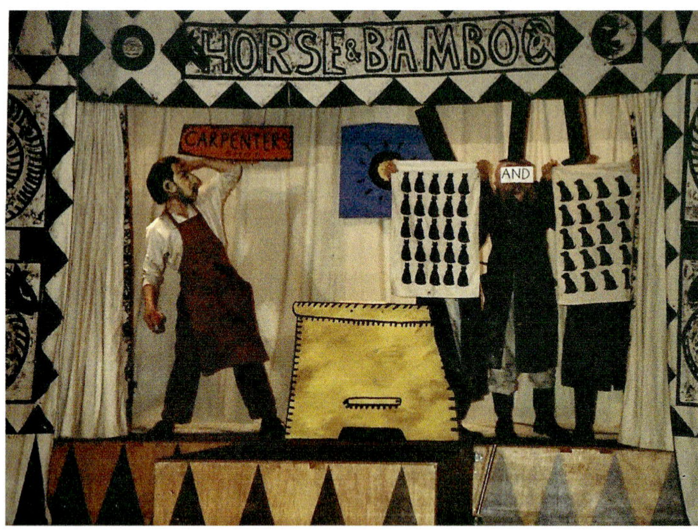
HORSE&BAMBOO
CARPENTERS
AND

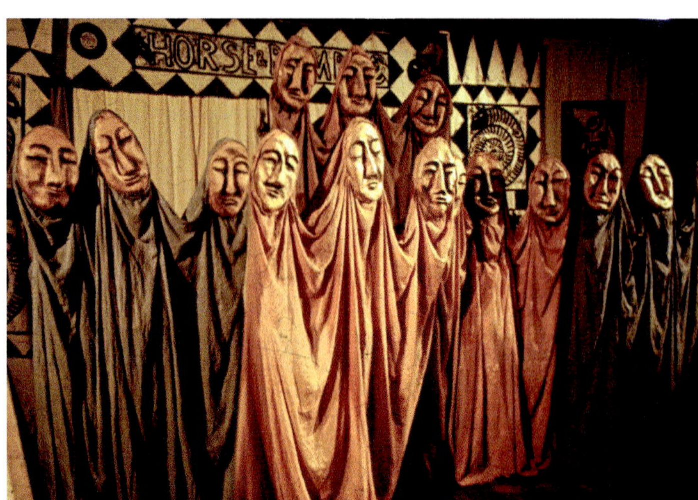

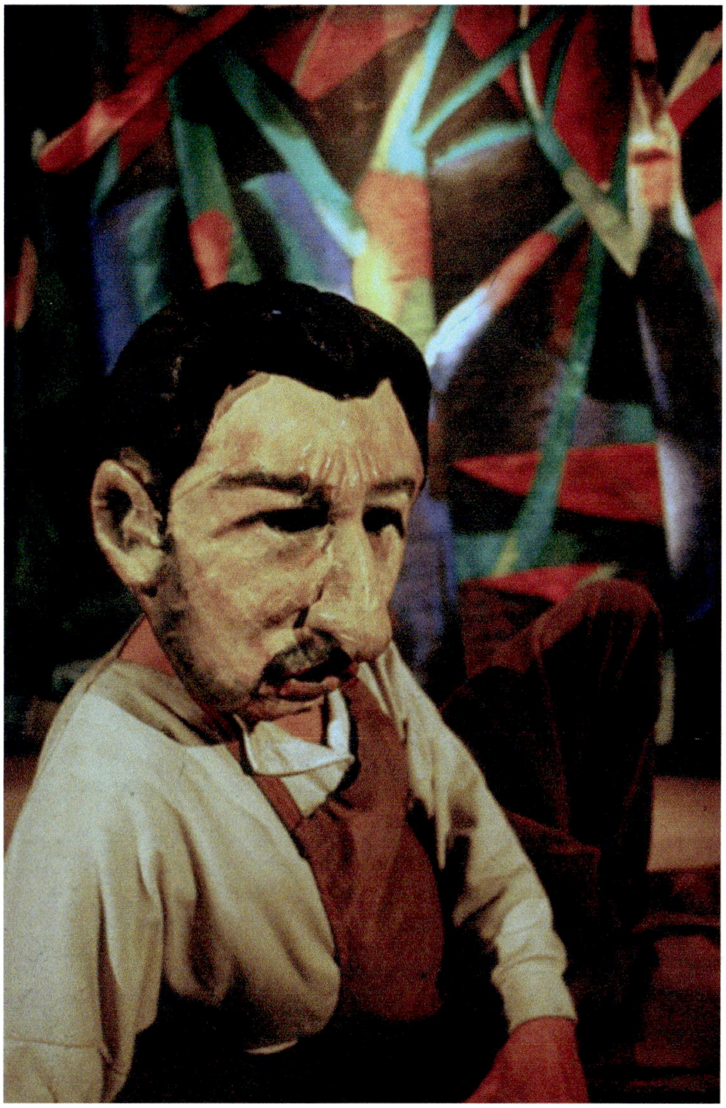

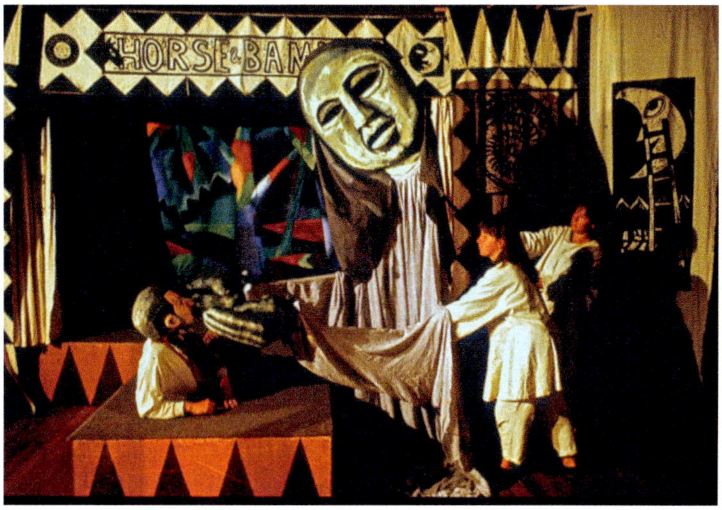
HORSE&BAM

18. A STRANGE (& UNEXPECTED) EVENT!, 1992

One day, mooching around Edinburgh, I found a shop that imported Mexican folk art; full of amazing and colourful objects at what I thought were bargain prices. I bought some papier-mache carnival masks, cheap tin images, and a beautiful ceramic Tree of Life. Investigating the background to these I came across the name of Jose Guadalupe Posada. He was the illustrator whose woodcuts have become the template for many Mexican folk images. Even today, long after his death, his imagery is vastly popular in Mexico. They provide much of the visual backdrop for The Day of The Dead.

J.G.Posada

After some dark, serious shows I felt that it was time to make a fun show. Something with humour, colour and energy. The idea came to write a story that imagined Posada's soul returning on All Souls Day – The Day of the Dead. I pictured that he would launch into an epic tussle with the Devil in front of our eyes. It would be a kind of Mexican Tom and Jerry, involving giant mousetraps, huge mallets, explosions and all sorts of surreal mayhem. Throughout, the source of the imagery we used would, wherever possible, be taken from Posada's own work. In the last scene Posada and the Devil drink *pulque* together. They become gradually more inebriated and slowly melt into each other's arms. So, the Day of the Dead comes to its end, at least until next year - *A Strange (and Unexpected) Event!*

One outcome of this idea was that we needed a raised stage. This way we could create an underworld from which both Posada and the Devil would emerge through trapdoors. Of course this also meant a big job setting it up at every venue, as the staging sections were extremely heavy. We put together a great group of musicians – Loz Kaye, Stu Barker (who went on to direct the music for many *Kneehigh* shows), plus Mary Keith and Claire Ingleheart, who doubled as performers. They formed a strong core to build the show around – and we were further helped by having Anne and Brad back with us from Canada. We toured the show with a team that was eleven strong.

The show was a riot, and went down really well everywhere we went. The tour started in May, in Kent, then travelled in mid-June to the North-East. It was one of our most popular shows, and we decided to keep it going the next year. The devil was a great character, really popular with audiences. Over the tours it was played by three very different performers – Mafalda da Camera, Nicky Fearn, Ursula Burns. Each gave it their own brilliant interpretation. In each case the Devil was a big hit. A fitting rival to Posada himself (played by Brad Harley and later by Jo King).

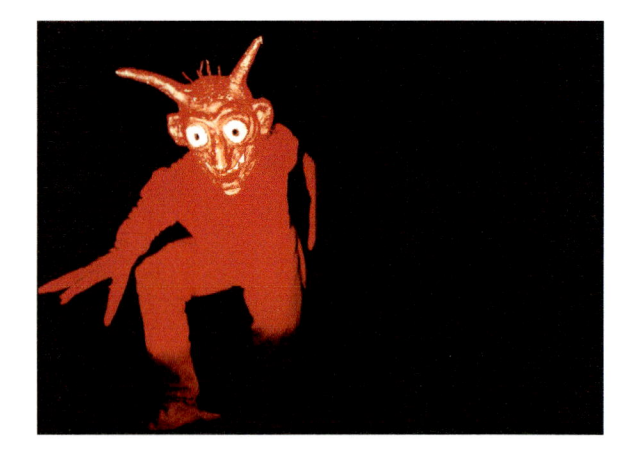

HORSE & BAMBOO THEATRE PRESENT
¡A STRANGE (AND UNEXPECTED) EVENT!

¡AMAZING PUPPETS MASKS AND MUSIC!

(THE LIFE & DEATH OF J.G. POSADA)

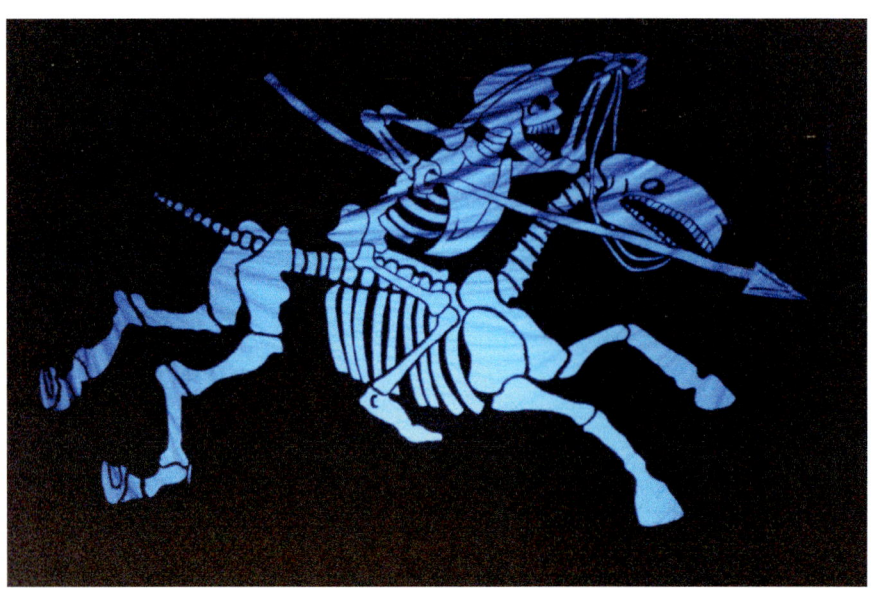

Scenes from A Strange (and Unexpected) Event!
Top right: Neville Cann
Bottom right: Stu Barker

Hungary

In 1993 we took the show to Eastern Europe, and walked from the Ukrainian border, travelling south through Hungary and skirting Debrecen before finishing the tour close to Kecskemét. It was one of our greatest horse-drawn adventures.

One of our performers and a good friend, Tim Bender, had married a Hungarian woman, Erika Szabo, a stewardess he met on his first flight to Budapest. Tim and Erika promptly set about arranging a tour for the company. The first began at Záhony on the Great Plains at the Ukrainian border; then onwards south-west to Debrecen and finally to villages in the area of Kecskemét. We had to hire Hungarian horses as British horses would inevitably wander over to the other side of the road, being left-hand drive animals (true). The shaft and harnessing system is also different in Hungary, so along with the horse we needed to hire local carts and harness. Negotiating all of this was an exceptionally long drawn-out process, taking up most of the night with liberal shots of home distilled palinka. Luckily our cello player, Neville Cann, was also a fluent speaker of Hungarian, and satisfactory arrangements were usually agreed just before I passed out from alcohol poisoning.

One evening, having finished a performance and relaxing round the fire, a group of Hungarian artists visited us. One was the animator and film-maker Péter Szoboszlay from Kecskemét Film Studio. Péter enjoyed both our show and our company. He invited us to visit the film studios and meet members of his team. Eventually, he arranged for a small film crew to follow us, on and off, for the next two years. They came to England and filmed at our base in Rossendale, as well as in Westminster Abbey. Péter and his wife Ilona became our close friends. His partly animated documentary film about the company – *Maszkok, lovak, szekerek' (Masks, carts, horses)* – is a lovely and unique record of those years.

REVIEWS

"Horse + Bamboo Theatre played to packed and appreciative audiences…an outstandingly creative performance…remarkable production of 'A Strange (and Unexpected) Event – the Life and Death of J.G.Posada'…memorable for its sheer rich inventiveness, its visual power, its energy and dynamic …unforgettable."

The Herald

"This lives up to its title…diabolically inventive…touching a chord the West End wouldn't know existed…vivid Mexican colours exploding against the black backdrop, the stage miraculously transformed into a whole series of moving tableaux…haunting…inspired music."

The Guardian

Opposite page top: Mary Keith, Jo King and Stu Barker in Hungary
Other photographs from Strange (and Unexpected) Event!, 1992

103

104

19. WESTMINSTER ABBEY, 1994/96

One day I received a letter from a Dr. Anthony Harvey, Canon of Westminster Abbey. He had been at a dinner-party in Kent, with a friend, the Governor of the Bank of England, when the guests heard that a horse-drawn theatre company was performing in the local village hall. With an evening to spare, some of the guests decided to catch the show. It happened to be *A Strange (& Unexpected) Event!* I wasn't there that evening, but I'm told that the company was invited back afterwards for showers and sherry.

It turned out that one of Canon Harvey's many responsibilities was coordinating the Westminster Good Friday events; in other words the celebration of the Passion of Christ within the parish of Westminster – which happens to include Westminster Abbey, Westminster Cathedral, the Houses of Parliament, Methodist Central Hall, and New Scotland Yard. He said that he was disappointed in the way the events had been staged recently and, after seeing our show, he wondered if I could come up with something better.

From this came a relationship with Westminster Abbey that lasted several years. On various occasions I also met with representatives from Westminster Cathedral and Central Hall. Things always had to be agreed between the Anglicans, Catholics and Methodists, and it wasn't always easy. One of the main concerns was the use of large puppets to represent Christ. In the Spanish *Semana Santa* parades (which I loved) floats or *tronos* usually carry a representation of the Virgin or Christ and I suggested something similar.

A large puppet of Christ would require three people to carry and manipulate it, as my plan was to stop at various points on route and quickly set up 'icons' based on the Stations of the Cross. In other words, we would tell the Easter story as a simple visual drama.

Problems arose around the puppet representing Christ, even if it was ten foot high. Each of the Christian denominations had a slightly different take on it. The Anglicans were generally relaxed about the idea; the Catholics were adamant that no female puppeteers should be used in this process; and it seemed to me that the Methodists weren't entirely happy about the use of visual imagery at all. I had to argue the case on several occasions, but finally it was agreed that we could go ahead, so long as it wasn't a woman puppeteer inside the body of the puppet Christ.

Otherwise things went smoothly. We hired the old hospital at Calderstones, near Whalley, to build the puppets, and Dr. Harvey travelled up to view our progress. On Good Friday the procession was led by the Dean and Canons of the Abbey, Cardinal Hume, and the Methodist Minister from Central Hall; it involved hundreds of people carrying printed woodcut banners, each with a single word that evoked the Easter story. In a surreal touch, we stopped outside New Scotland Yard to receive a blessing from the Chief Constable, and then a huge number of motorcycle police outriders accompanied us past the Houses of Parliament.

Once back inside the Abbey Horse & Bamboo performed an updated version of Angel Mummers, an old show from 1980. Having the keys to the Abbey overnight in order to rehearse the piece was quite an experience. It meant having the run of the place, wandering around tombs of kings and queens while the technical crew gaffer-taped cables to historic memorial grave stones.

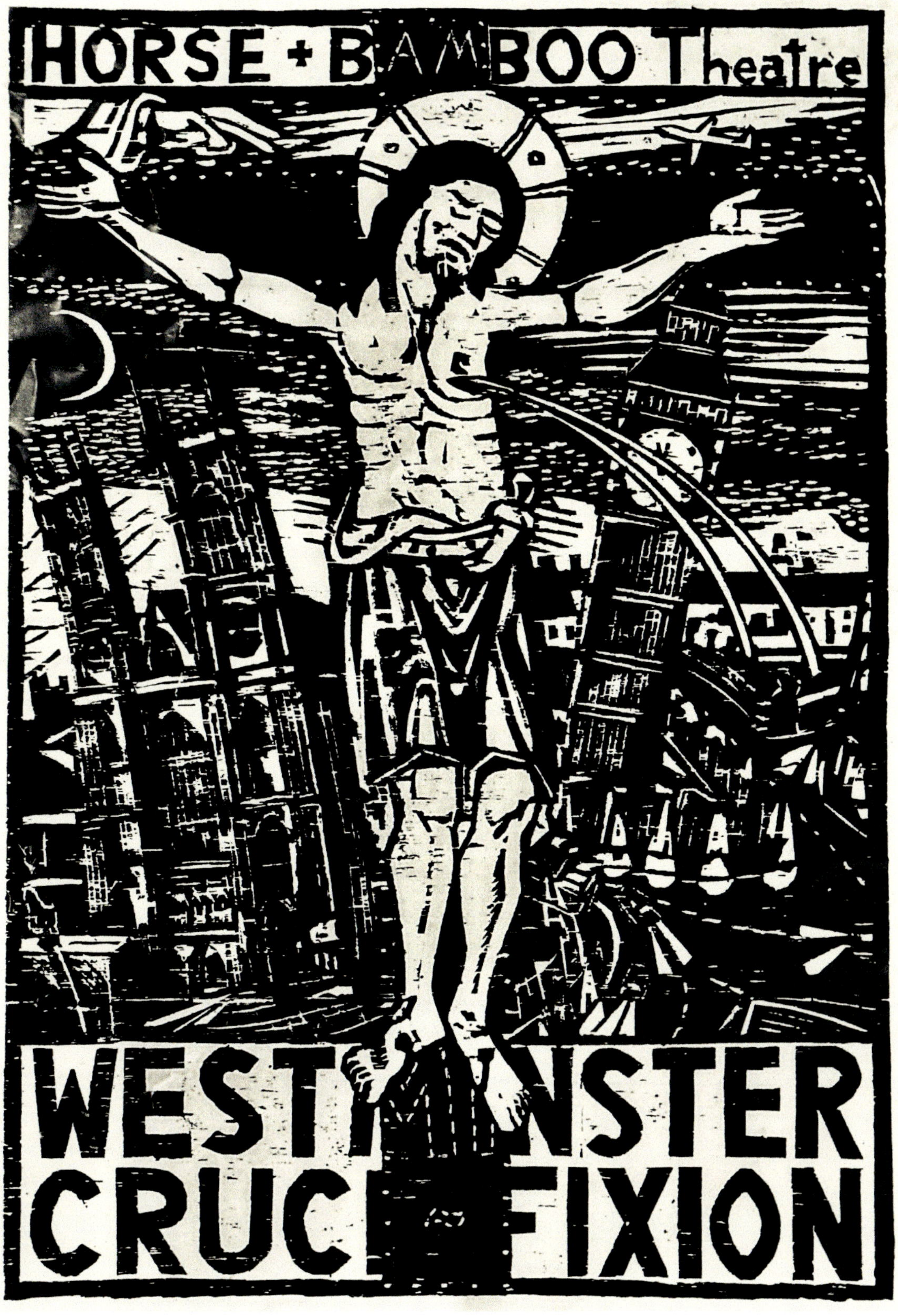
HORSE + BAMBOO Theatre
WESTMINSTER
CRUCIFIXION

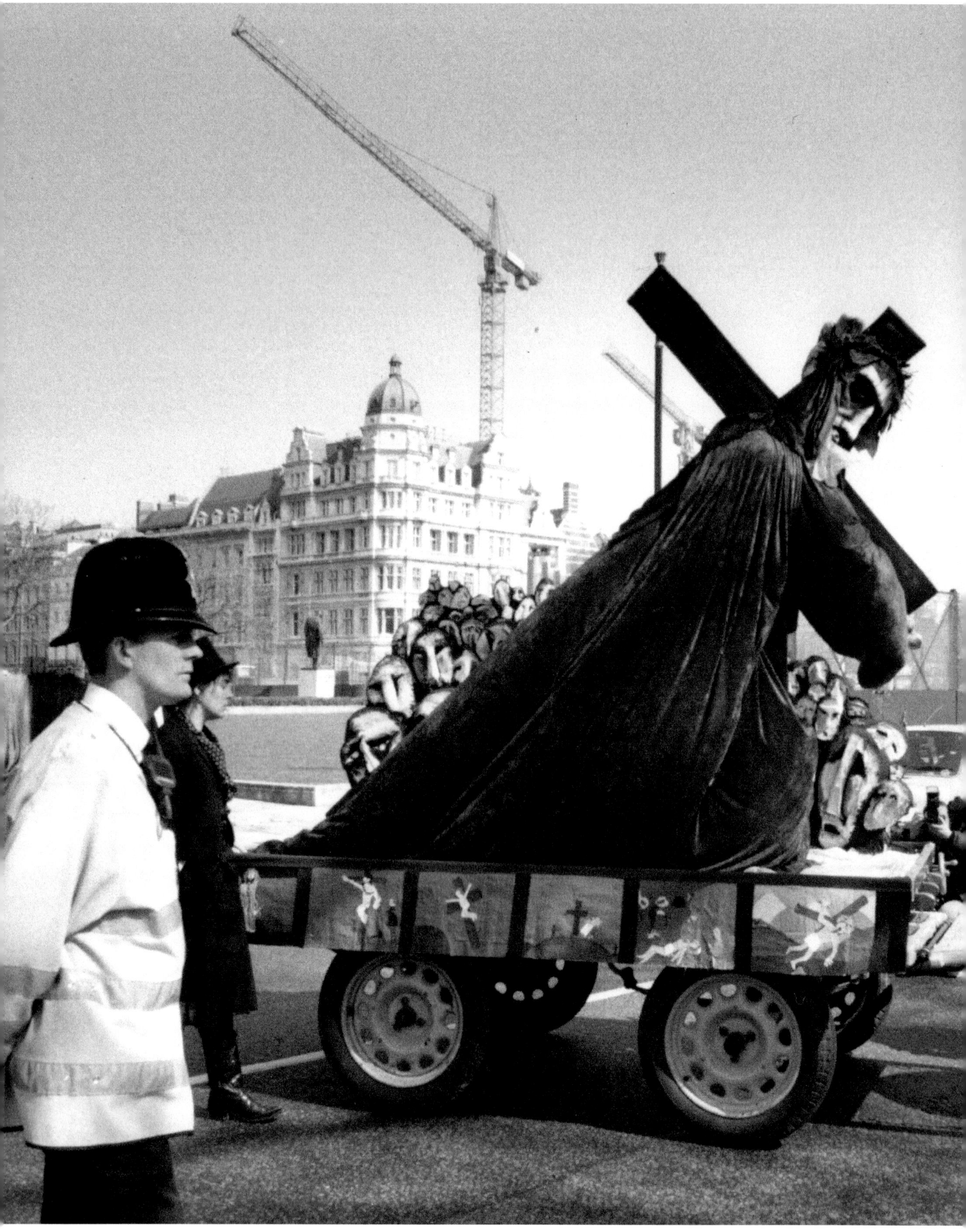

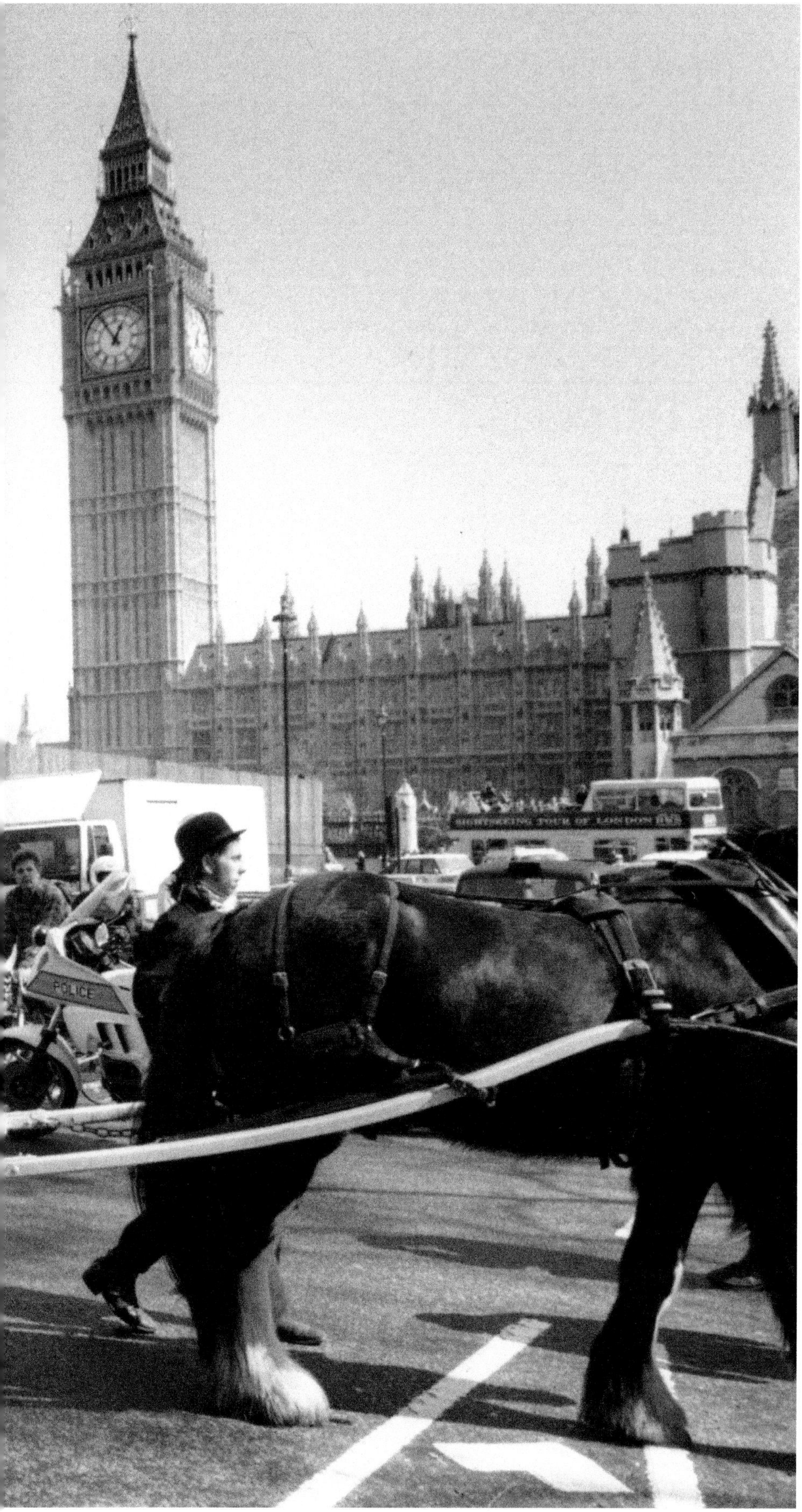
POLICE

1996

These Easter events were a success, and photographs of our Christ puppet made the front pages of the next days' papers. We were invited back in 1996 to create a second Good Friday event. This time we brought our horses and built small versions of Spanish *tronos* on our carts. The horses had the honour of being stabled overnight in Westminster Abbey. I saw the Dean out early in the morning, shovelling up the horse's droppings, "Good for the roses", he told me with a smile. We also brought a large group of musicians and a choir to accompany the parade and perform outside the Abbey.

Inside the Abbey we performed an adapted version of *A Strange (& Unexpected) Event!*. This also caused a commotion, with several newspapers suggesting that it was 'inappropriate' as it celebrated the Day of the Dead resurrection of a left-wing artist (J.G. Posada). The issue was labelled 'a political storm' in the press and even featured in the BBC Radio4 comedy News Quiz that week. The Daily Telegraph ran an item headed 'Abbey goes Left-wing for Easter'. The Ven. George Austin, Archdeacon of York, was reported as saying "Nothing surprises me about the Church of England these days."

In 1997, partly as a thank you for overseeing the two Easter parades, we were asked to perform *Visions of Hildegard* as the Abbey's regular Sunday Service. 700 people were in the congregation, and the company were introduced from the pulpit by Anthony Harvey. At the end of a very memorable show, I was surprised and delighted to see the congregation stand and applaud.

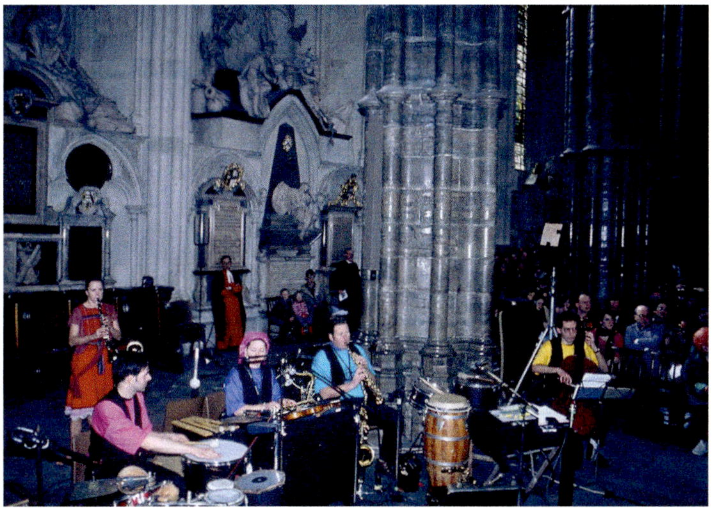

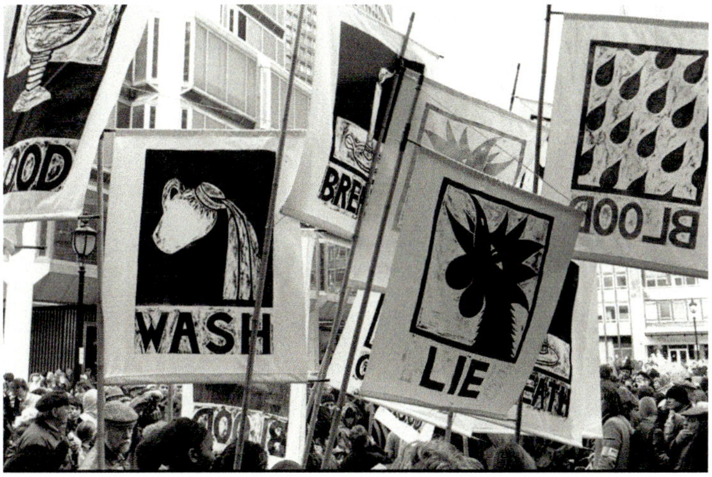
WASH
LIE

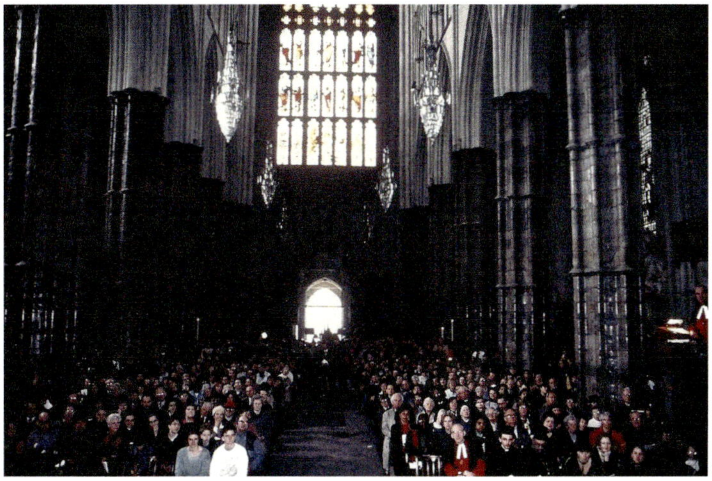

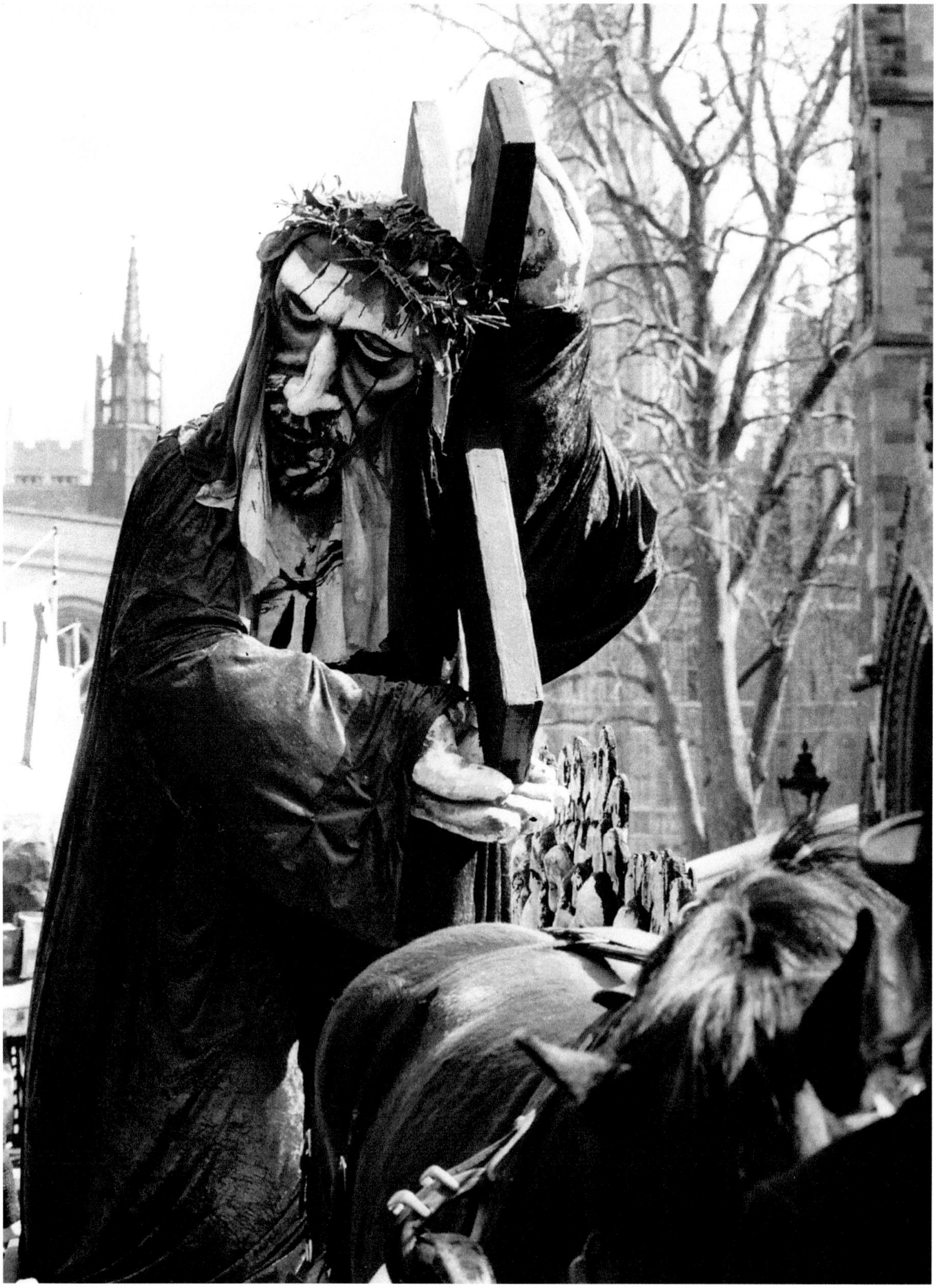

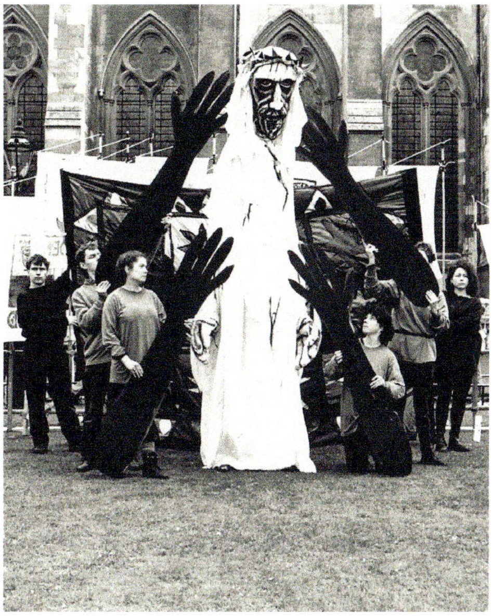

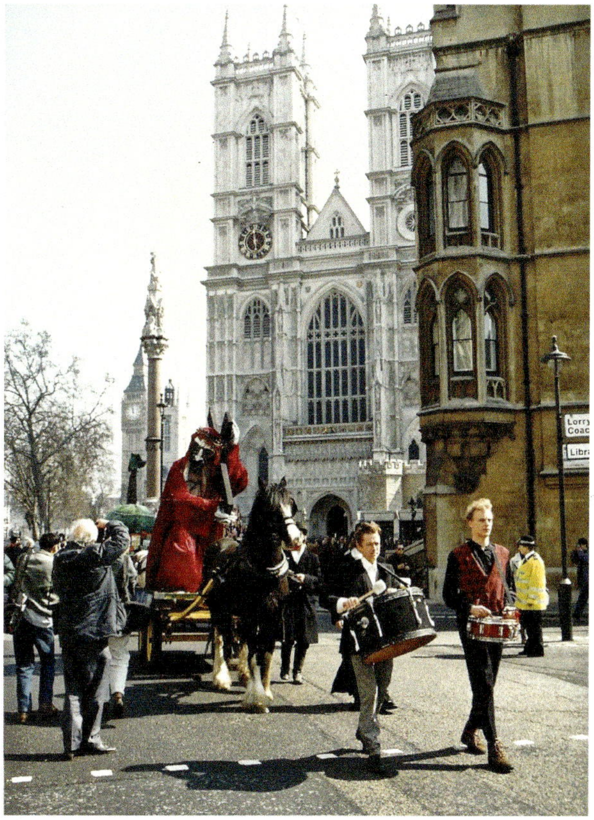

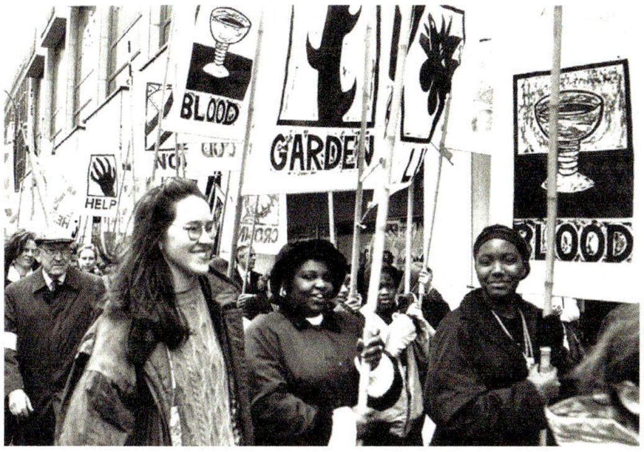
BLOOD
GARDEN
HELP
BLOOD

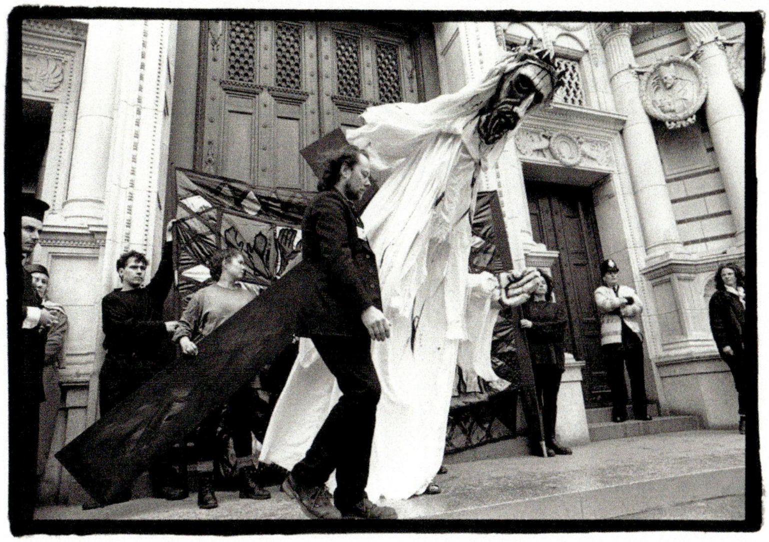

20. DANCE OF WHITE DARKNESS, 1994

Emboldened by setting the Devil loose above the altar at Westminster Abbey, our next project was to dramatise the story of Maya Deren. Deren is an important figure in the history of alternative cinema in the USA, but what first attracted my attention was her book *The Voodoo Gods* (originally called The Divine Horsemen). I first read it in the early 1970s, the story of Deren's journey to Haiti, to film voudon dance. This venture took her on an unplanned inner journey that resulted in her becoming a mambo, a voudon priestess. The book is also a critique of modern western beliefs and morals, which Deren compares negatively with the integrity and cooperation that she experienced among the serviteurs (sèvitè), the followers of voudon with whom she came to live and work.

I was feeling increasingly confident in what we could achieve on stage. In *Dance of White Darkness* I dropped any caution. The story attempted to explore voudon ceremonies, the loa spirit world, and spirit possession on stage. The story also looked at the relationship between these things and the 'tourist voodoo' that Deren writes about and comments on in her book.

One problem was to find performers who could interpret the material. Not so much the Maya Deren character herself, who was on a journey of discovery as a sophisticated American artist in an alien world. The real difficulty was finding performers to play the Haitian villagers and sèvitè. They would be the participants in the voudon ceremonies. Despite making an enormous effort I found it impossible to find experienced Afro-Caribbean performers. We contacted the Gambian/Senegalese master drummer Lamin Jassey and his wife, Vicky. Culturally there are very close links between West Africa and Haitian voudon. Vicky joined the touring company and Lamin and Vicky together worked with us to train the performers in voudon ceremonies and dance. We also had help from the choreographer T.C. Howard, from Ludus dance. It was a big regret that we couldn't find any other Haitian, West Indian or African performers at that period. I asked the Chair of our Board, Erik Knudsen, who is half Ghanaian, if he felt that we should abandon the project because of this. Erik was adamant that we should continue.

HORSE & BAMBOO THEATRE

DANCE OF
WHITE DARKNESS
(Maya and the Horsemen)

The tour

The show became *Dance of White Darkness*. This was a phrase used by Maya Deren in her book to describe spirit possession. This is when a sèvitè is gripped by a trance in which their body is taken over, possessed, by a voudou spirit, or loa. Another key image that I used in our show was taken from the same passage in Deren's book – that of the horse and rider. The idea here is that the body of the sèvitè becomes the mount for a loa. It was a potentially difficult subject to depict well.

When we performed the show at Atlantic College, the international college in South Wales, I was approached by a member of college staff after the show. He introduced me to a young woman, who turned out to be a Haitian student. She asked if we could speak alone. She then asked me 'how do you know these things?' She told me that on leaving Haiti her family said that she should never talk about her religion. Yet, here we were, an English theatre company in a Welsh college, dealing with what she assumed were strongly taboo subjects here. She assumed that I must have lived in Haiti.

We spent ten weeks in preparation and rehearsal, and a couple more weeks on previews. Then we packed, and the company of nine (and our horses) were ready at the beginning of July. The show toured to Dumfries & Galloway, Cumbria, Lancashire, Yorkshire and Humberside. Later we took the show to the Netherlands. During the 1990s we had a wonderful Dutch agency – Drie Stenen – who produced highly successful, and profitable, tours for several years.

Orkney and Eastern Europe

In 1995 we started a second tour of the show in Caithness. After this we travelled south, and eventually hooked up with a ship to Orkney, as part of the St. Magnus Festival. On Orkney we walked to the island of South Ronaldsay. This was the community that had been deeply affected by what was known as the 'Orkney child abuse scandal'. In this, children had been removed from their families in dawn raids, and taken into care. All charges had been dismissed by the time we arrived, including the original charges of 'satanic abuse'. But children had been separated from their families for over a year, and it had caused enormous suffering.

On our arrival on the island, the authorities got to hear more about the subject of the show. There was concern as to what the implications of this might be. Young people were excluded from the opening night and the show was watched nervously by councillors and counsellors. At the end the show was pronounced 'safe'. It was a brave, though an entirely correct, conclusion, and any suggestion of censorship was avoided. The Orkney tour then went ahead successfully.

After Orkney we took the show to Roma settlements in Slovakia. Then, later, to refugee groups on the Hungarian border areas with Croatia and Serbia. Refugees were pouring over the border to escape the war, and we performed in centres where young people affected by the conflict were gathering to meet one another.

This was our second Hungarian tour and was part funded by UNHCR. It was an extraordinary situation for us. But we felt that we were playing a useful part simply by being there with our show, improvising parades and entertainment for the locals and the younger refugees. What we didn't know at the time was that, caught up in the instability of the conflict zone, a number of promises to pay us for this work were broken.

On this leg of the tour we were given the great iron key to the large medieval hilltop castle in Siklós, which had been made available for our exclusive use. Siklós is the most southerly town in Hungary, and just two miles from the Croatian border. Once across the castle moat and after pushing open the huge creaky wooden door, we each chose our own medieval hall as a bedroom, and then met together on the roof. Here we would eat and drink at night whilst observing the mortar fire arcing through the sky, as people were trying to kill one another just a few miles to the south.

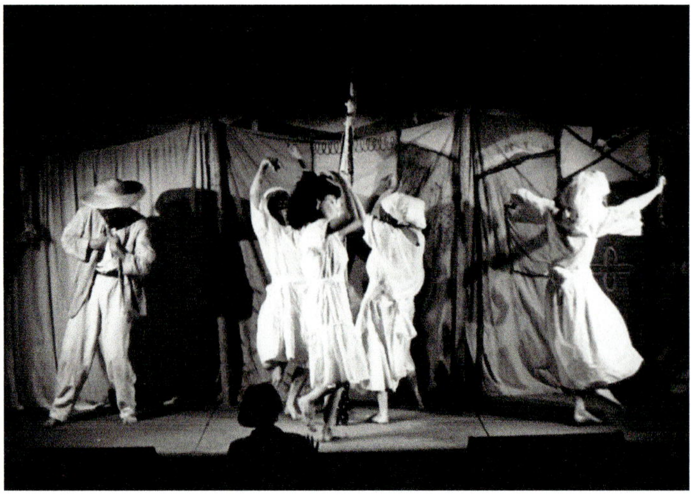
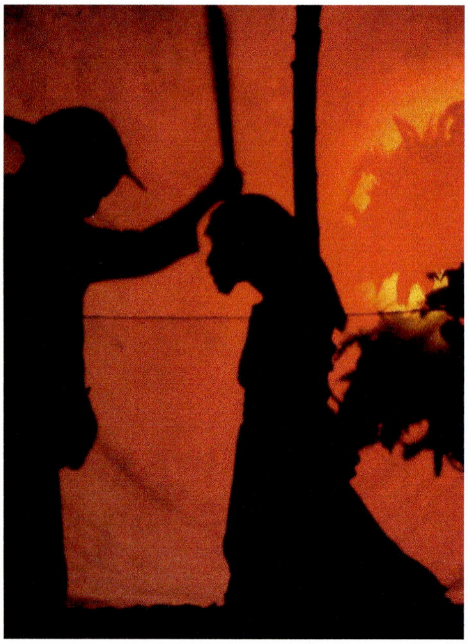
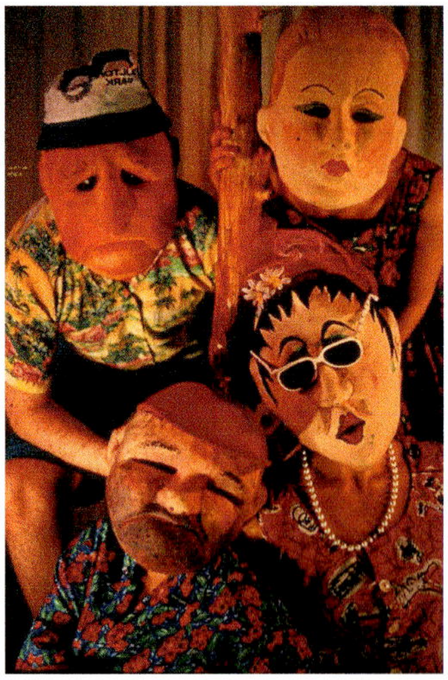
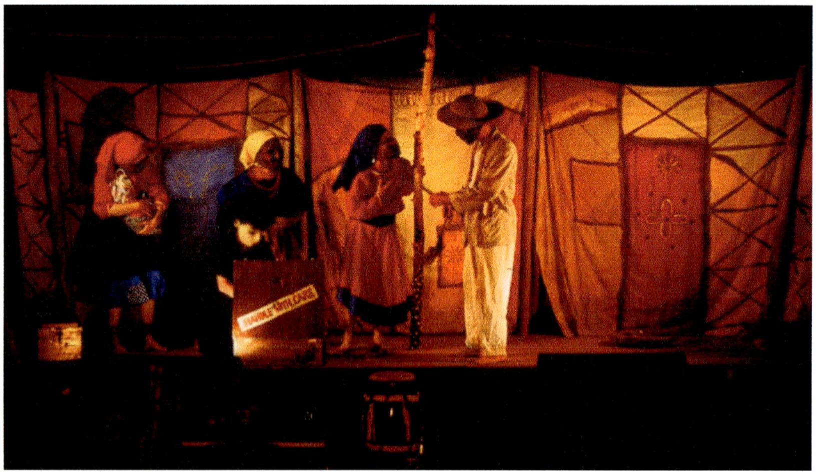
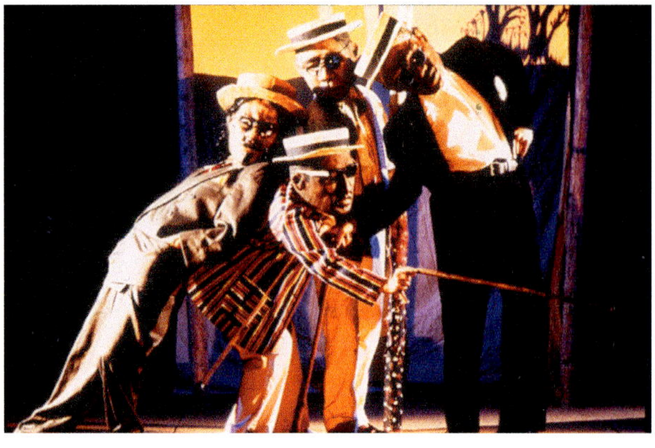

In nearby Villány I met a wine-maker who had just had his ancestral wine-estate returned to him decades after it had been confiscated by the communist state. He turned up at our campsite when I was alone enjoying a siesta. He woke me, and insisted that I come along with him to celebrate his good fortune. We walked through the village, then through an entrance into a green hillside covered in vines. Next we went underground, through the wooden doors into earth caverns that seemed to go on and on. Each was full of giant wooden barrels. Every so often he would climb a ladder, open a barrel, and fill a glass for me. Villány is rightly famed for its wine, and his feelings at having this wine empire returned to him could only be guessed at. In any case I spoke almost no Hungarian; he knew no English. As we went further and further underground, large banqueting tables appeared as if in a dream, each lit by the feeble electric lights that were strung throughout the caves. The wine kept flowing; everything looked pre-war; was dusty, cobwebby and totally untouched since the revolution.

I remember turning up at the campsite with the biggest headache I've ever known. The rest of the company had now returned, and I introduced my new friend to them before collapsing into my tent to sleep it off. A few days later, on our last night in the town he threw a party for us all in his palace inside the hill.

REVIEW:

…Horse + Bamboo have translated Deren's story with great integrity into a theatre piece in which all the performers wear expressive masks. Maya Deren arrives in Haiti as one of a group of tourists. She lodges in the house of one of the islanders and thus come into contact with 'voodoo'. In nine short acts the changes in Deren are accurately portrayed by the company. From the observation of 'voodoo' trinkets sold for money, via an attempt to capture Haiti as it really is by living with the locals, to the moment she is forced to choose between returning home, her task incomplete, or becoming a member of the community from which position it would be impossible to film.

The company consistently hit upon small details which communicate the changes in Deren better than the use of spectacular effects would. Only the tourists and their masks are caricatures. Deren and the Haitians have eloquently sculpted masks which contribute to a sense of realism rather than distract from it. The vodoun apparitions were created in simple but enormously effective ways; never frightening; sometimes stunningly beautiful – the spiritual world of vodoun is made visible.

The music, which was performed live, was integral to the performance. It carried one along and without exaggeration could be said to form the stage for the performers. I can't think of a better compliment! It is also no exaggeration to say that Horse + Bamboo, by telling Deren's story in this way, have achieved what she herself failed to do, namely to capture a lifelike impression of Haitian spiritual life.

Maarten Jansen trans. Elke Deadman.

21. VISIONS OF HILDEGARD, 1994-6

I mapped out an idea for the next show in 1993 – the story of Hildegard of Bingen, the revered 12th century Benedictine abbess and mystic whose extraordinary and groundbreaking music was in the process of being rediscovered. I had first come across this remarkable woman several years before, when reading Dr. Oliver Sacks first book *Migraine*, in which he considers her visions to be part of a migrainous syndrome.

By the time we got round to planning the show, however, the company was undergoing a financial crisis. We were struggling with the impact of the financial losses of the Hungarian tour of 1994. We needed to drastically cut back our costs, and create a touring show that could earn income with little or no financial risk. Drastic decisions were taken – to cut the touring company from seven or eight to four performers including just one musician, Claire Ingleheart, and most dramatically of all, to trim the rehearsal period from eight to three weeks. We all worked hard to make this succeed, but there's no doubt that the early Hildegard shows were drastically under-rehearsed. There was nothing that we could do about it as the tour had already been planned and contracted. The issue was simply a lack of rehearsal time.

Over the first month of touring the cast worked heroically at every available hour to improve the situation. I travelled whenever possible to meet up with them so that we could spend time together working to deal with the weaknesses in the show. Eventually we had a four day gap while in the Midlands, and the company agreed to give up their break for a concerted period of rehearsal. We hired the village hall in Ansty, and worked hard to bring the show up to something like our usual standard. It made a big difference. After that things improved rapidly, and gradually *Visions of Hildegard* blossomed into a rich and successful show.

VISIONS OF HILDEGARD

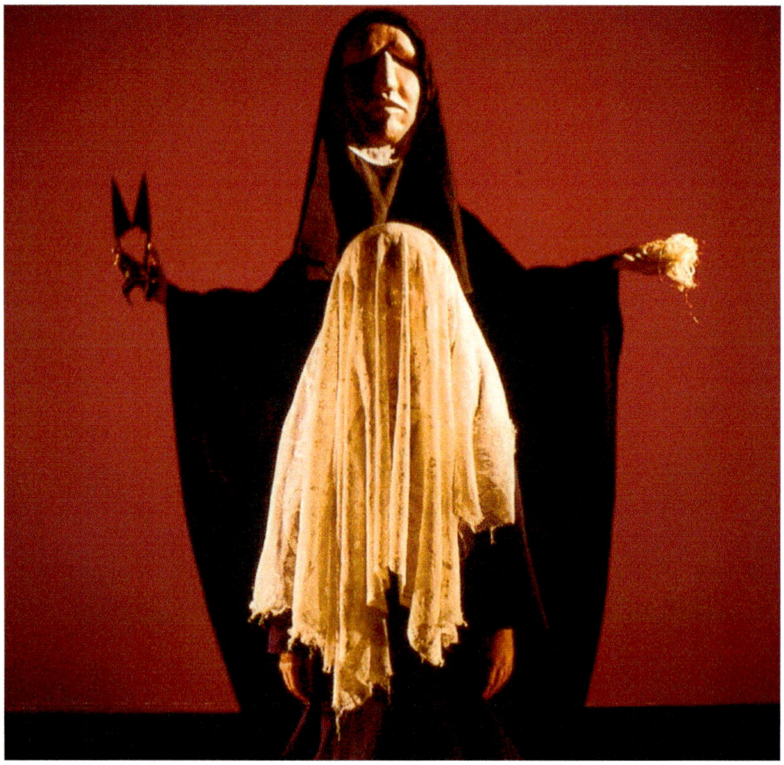

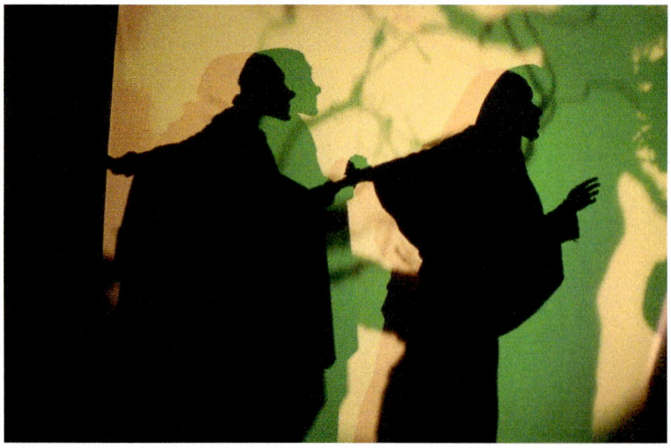

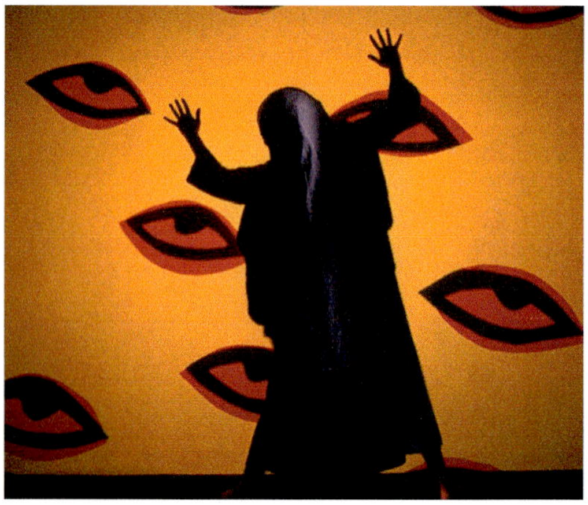

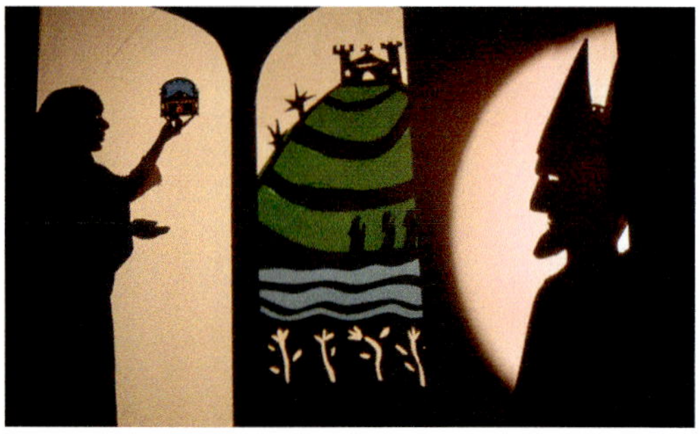

Rehearsing with puppets always requires time. In my experience it will take two or three times longer to rehearse a puppet or mask scene when compared to working with actors. There's also the time required to make the puppets and masks. The visual side of the production was, of course, a large part of what the company was about.

To compensate for having a small cast we used a complex arrangement of shadow projections for *Visions of Hildegard*. In many ways the show was very filmic, as hand-held lamps were carefully moved through and around detailed models backstage to create large projected shadow images of castles, landscapes, the River Rhine, and life in the abbey. Best of all they lent themselves to recreating Hildegard's extraordinary colourful visions, and these gave a distinctive and unique character to the production.

In May 1996 we gave ourselves another four weeks to re-work the show; longer than the whole of the original rehearsal period. This time we were properly prepared and the tour went well from the start. So when we were asked by Westminster Abbey to put on a full show as a Sunday service, we decided that *Visions of Hildegard* was the obvious choice. We brought in a large band of musicians to accompany the performance, which worked brilliantly in the Abbey. To my surprise the Abbey decided to use the show as their regular Sunday service. It was a memorable show – to a packed Abbey congregation as the sun slowly set behind the stained glass windows.

22. THE LEGEND OF THE CREAKING FLOORBOARD, 1997

After writing a series of shows about historical characters, it felt like time for a new approach. An inspiration was Lol Coxhill's 1976 recording on his album *Diverse*. On the first side of the record there's an improvised piece for soprano saxophone and a loose floorboard.

The Legend of the Creaking Floorboard had clear references to the tale of Orpheus and Eurydice – Orpheus in the Underworld. I also wanted to try working with big, formalised masks worn above the head. The performers look out of a gauze window at the neck level of the characters. I had used this type of mask before, so I knew that it would demand a highly stylised performance. It results in the masked figures moving more like a large puppet than an actor or dancer. In contrast to the high female figures, for much of the performance the male figure would be a bunraku-type puppet, operated by three puppeteers, and it was half life-size. Using three puppeteers invests this kind of puppet with an unusual power, as if it funnels three times the energy and presence into a single puppet character. The set was designed and made by myself and Colette Garrigan. Work started in April; rehearsals at the end of May, and the first show would be on 17th June. We put aside seven weeks for rehearsal, not wanting to repeat the problems we'd had with *Visions of Hildegard*.

In *The Legend of the Creaking Floorboard* the two main characters are twin sisters, Gog and Magog. At the start of the story they sit on their rocking chairs, both calmly knitting. But Gog, it turns out, has a lover, the Knife-grinder. He makes an unscheduled visit and invites her out, leaving Magog on her own for the evening. Magog is clearly a little put-out by this turn of events but she tries to relax. However, as she knits, her rocking chair disturbs a loose floorboard. The creak just gets louder and louder. The noise irritates her, and she tries to fix it by tapping the board gently with a hammer. But nothing works – the creaking gets louder and louder and finally, Magog explodes in a rage. Picking up the hammer she destroys the offending floorboard, smashing it into splinters. Out of control, she turns to the next one and then the next…wood flies everywhere….a huge hole appears in the floor. Only then does Magog stop and gape at the damage she has done. I loved the idea of destroying the stage in the first 10 minutes of the performance.

At that moment Gog and Knife-grinder return home. Astonished, all three stare into the hole in the middle of what had been their living room. Knife-grinder offers to look under the floor to assess the damage, and he gingerly lets himself down into the hole. When he reappears he asks the two sisters to pass him various tools and items. Each time he disappears below the floor for a few seconds longer. Increasingly fascinated by the underfloor world, he asks for his bicycle to be passed down to him. Gog remonstrates – she is getting nervous and worried, but the bicycle gets carefully passed into the floor. Knife-grinder ties one end of Magog's knitting wool to his handlebars. He reassures the sisters that he will keep a connection to the room above. As he cycles off under the stage, we see the wool unwinding on its knitting needle, slowly at first but getting faster and faster – until it comes to its end and flies off into the hole. The loose end promptly disappears below the floorboards, leaving Gog and Magog stranded and horrified at the turn of events.

At this point in the story there's a big change. The stage is invaded by a group of sweeping women – all with the same high head masks as Gog and Magog themselves. They sweep the stage, then totally transform it into a cavernous underworld. The story then continues with Gog's search for Knife-grinder in the Underworld. This, possibly the strangest of all Horse & Bamboo shows, was well received and toured for two years in the UK and the Netherlands.

HORSE & BAMBOO THEATRE
The Legend of the CREAKING FLOORBOARD

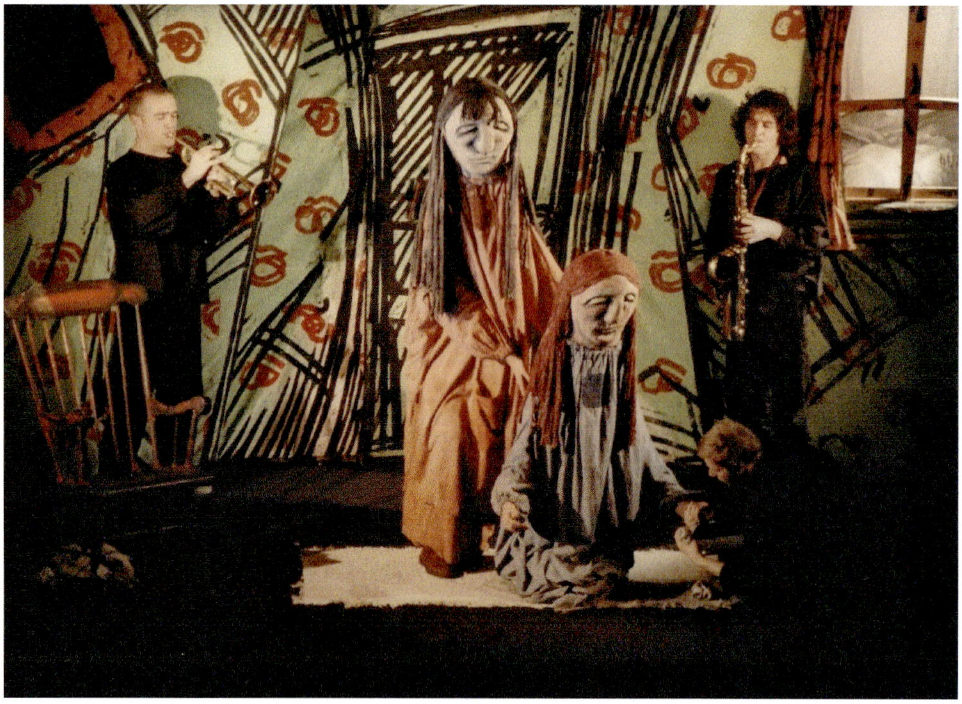

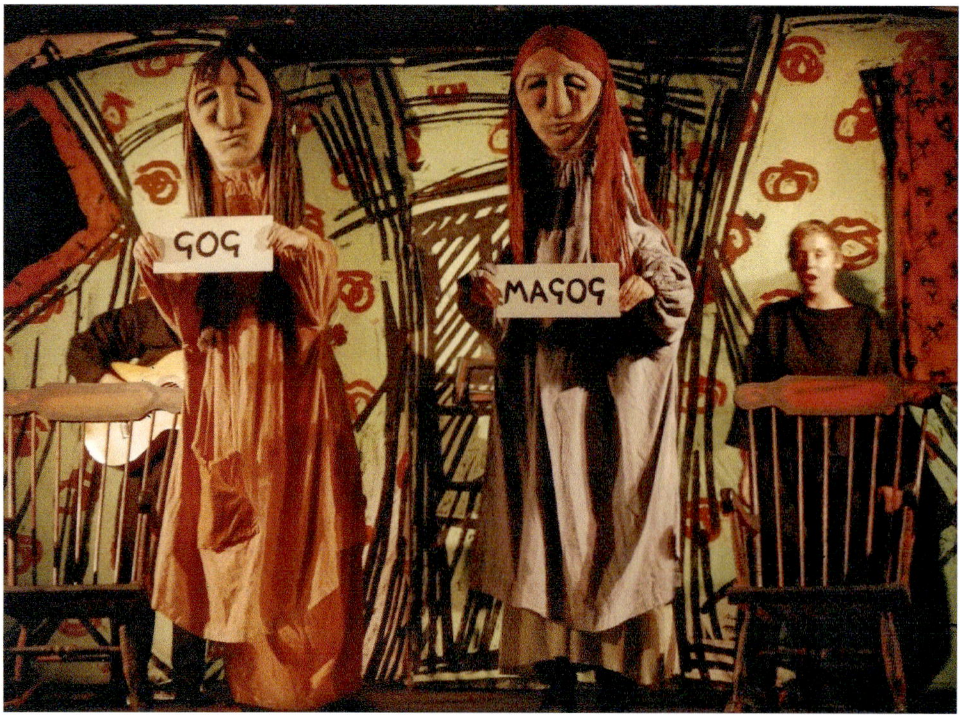
GOG
MAGOG

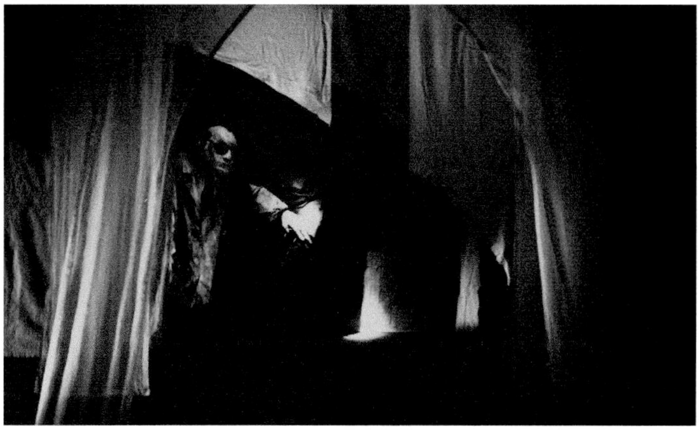

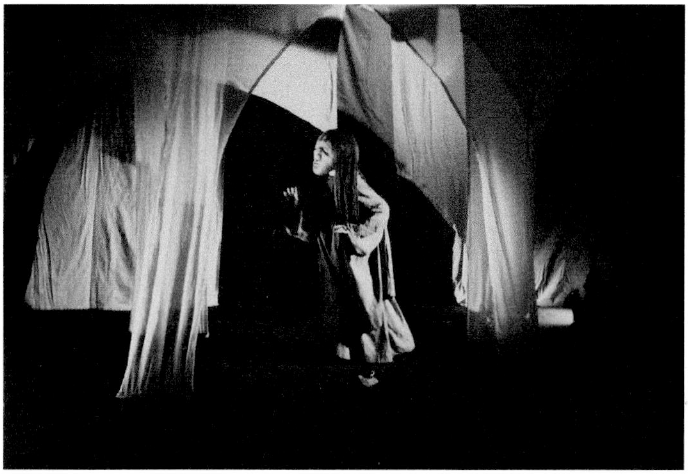

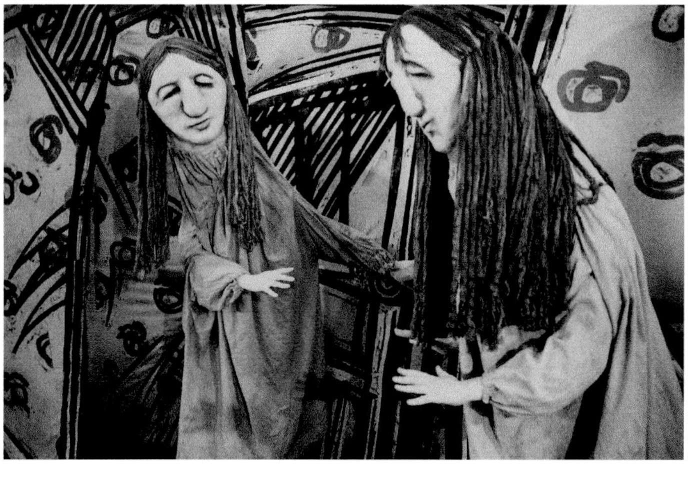

23. HARVEST OF GHOSTS, 1999

Professor Martin Banham, from the department of African Theatre Studies at the University of Leeds, telephoned to ask if he might bring over a visiting Commonwealth Fellow, Professor Sam Ukala, from Nigeria. Professor Ukala was researching English Folk Theatre and couldn't find any practitioners. Could we help?

Folkism

Dr. Sam Ukala visited shortly after we had moved into our new building in Waterfoot, and he was excited by what he saw of our rehearsals for *The Legend of the Creaking Floorboard*. Sam was Professor of Drama and Theatre Arts at Edo State University as well as being a renowned playwright in Nigeria. His area of special interest was an area that he termed 'folkism'; the study of native African forms of theatre, in contrast to the drama tradition that had been introduced to West Africa by the British colonial power. Native forms were at the heart of his own theatre writing. I read his work and found it unlike anything I had come across before, but powerful and strange. When I suggested that Leeds University might help him return to work with me on a new production he jumped at the opportunity. We kept in touch for over a year in order to organise the paperwork and funds to support his time in Britain. Communications with Nigeria were difficult and every letter sent took months before getting a reply.

Professor Ukala joined us in late 1998 and it was only then that we really began to consider just how we might actually work together. Communications with Nigeria had been so difficult since we last met that it just hadn't been possible over that year to have any proper dialogue as to how we would go about working jointly on a production. There was a period of shock in which Sam digested that our work was essentially non-verbal. He was an acclaimed playwright and words were his 'dominant tools'. We needed time to think about this potentially huge problem, plus there was also the matter of agreeing on what the subject would be.

I had recently been on tour in the Netherlands, and there I heard about the protests by Ijo campaigners about the devastation of the Nigerian Delta region by oil companies, in particular Shell. I mentioned this to Sam, and he immediately felt it would make a good starting point for us to work with. Sam had known the writer Ken Saro-Wiwa, who had been executed in 1995, along with eight others, for their involvement in this very protest. I suggested that Sam should write a dramatic treatment for us to use as a point of departure. The story of this process was recorded by Sam Ukala and published in *African Theatre: Playwrights & Politics* 2001.

HORSE + BAMBOO

STREETSTORY: 'HARVEST OF GHOSTS'
SAM UKALA / BOB FRITH

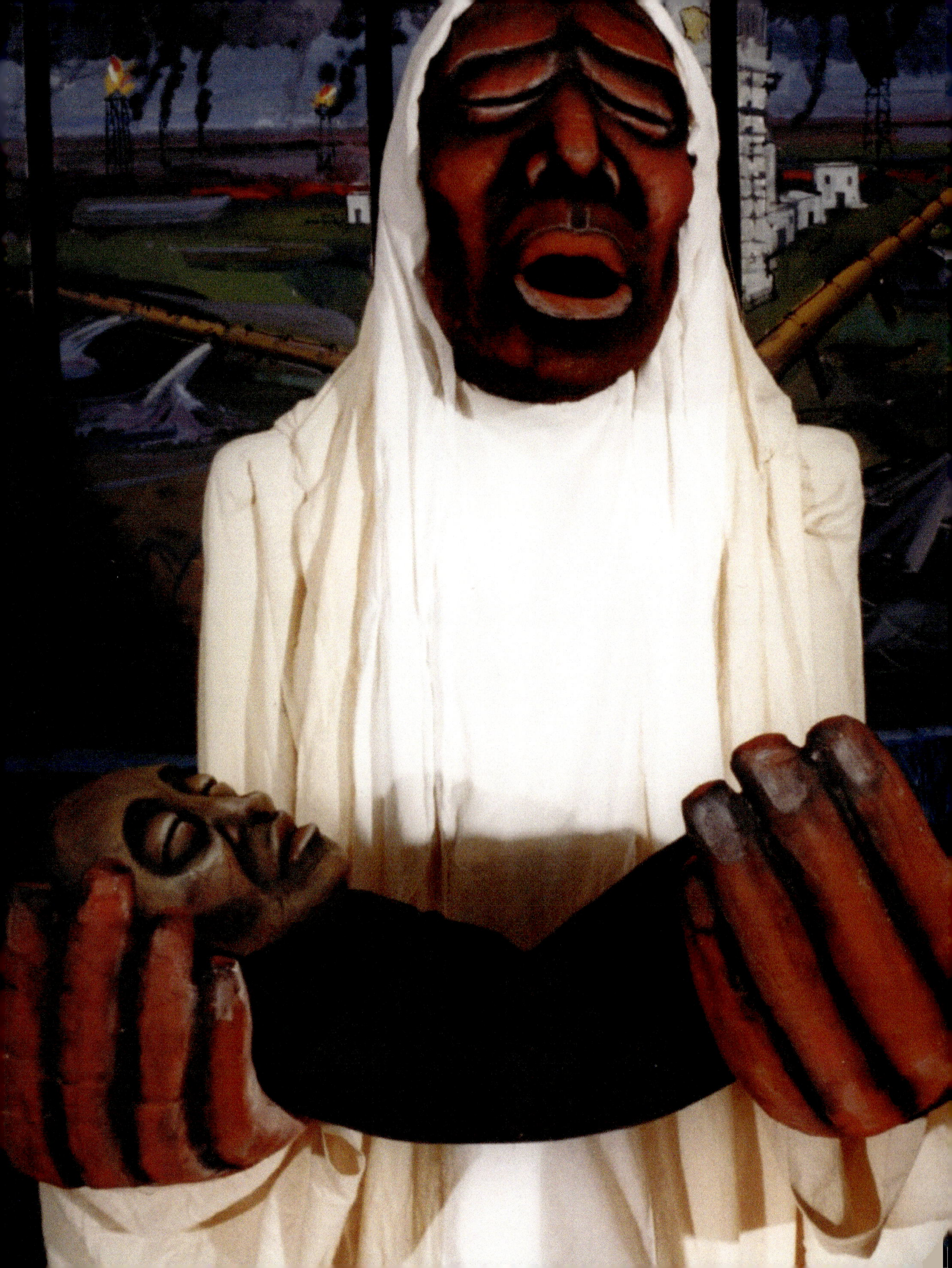

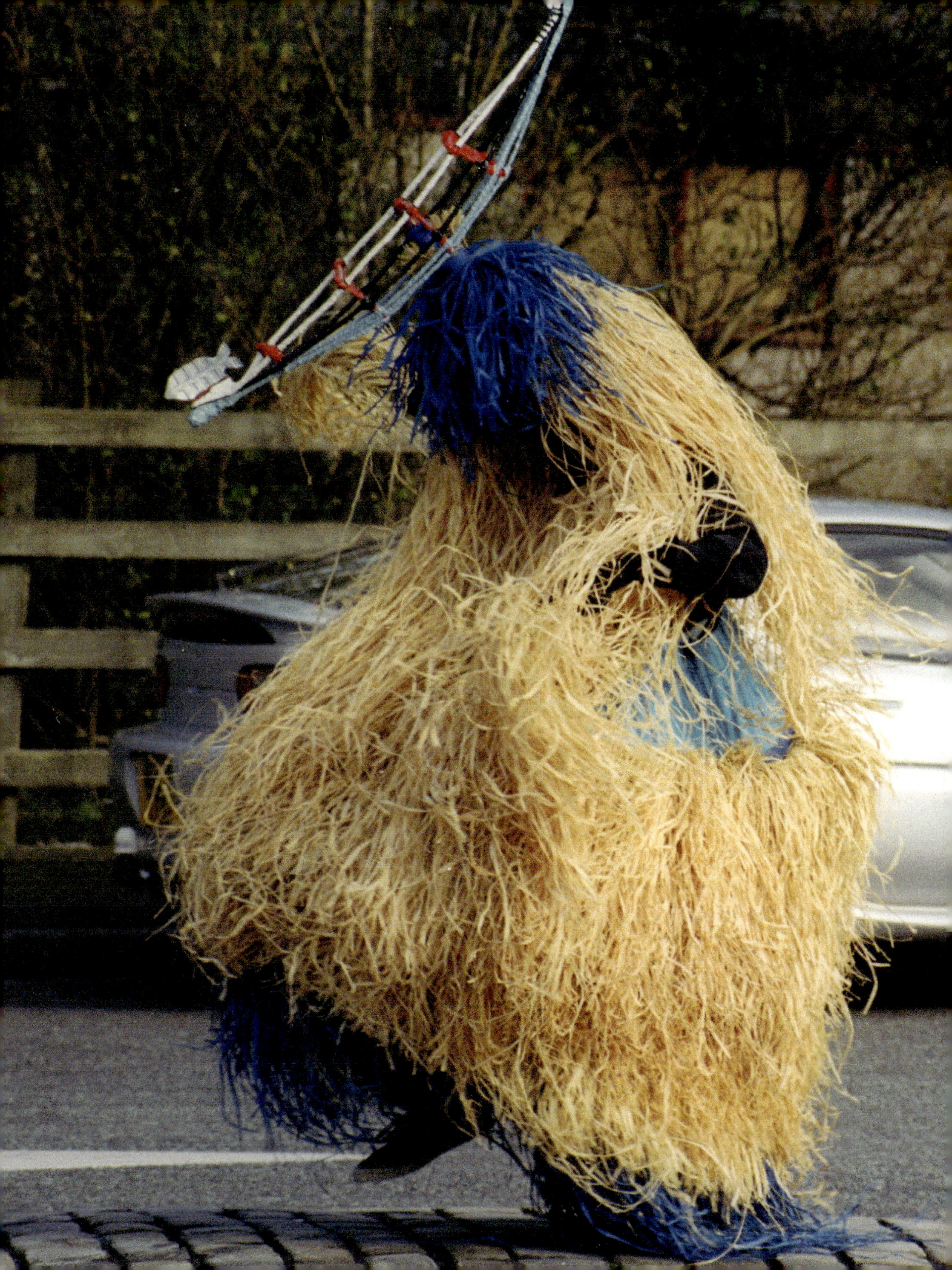

Casting

Sam locked himself away (he was staying with Kay and myself at our moorland farmhouse) and he wrote a scenario in five days. On reading it I immediately felt that it was absolutely right for us, and I quickly started the process of turning it into a visual script. This meant making a few small alterations to Sam's basic and highly political storyline but, in essence, very few changes were made. I simply created visual settings for his storyline. I also started work on designing a set, masks, puppets, and the various props. After that, working closely with Sam, we created a choreography that would enable his story to be told as if it were a dance piece. In retrospect it was extraordinary how smoothly 'Harvest of Ghosts' was put together, given our totally different perspectives on theatre. Our approaches and practice were quite different, since Sam's directing had mainly been with undergraduate students and text-based plays, mine had been with professional actors and performers experienced in visual and movement-based theatre. Sam therefore tended to be more prescriptive; I tended to allow room for experimentation and for input from the wider company.

We were far more successful in casting black performers than we had been in 1994 with *Dance of White Darkness*. It was essential to work with a mixed race cast for *Harvest of Ghosts* and we chose Dan Poyser, 'Funmi Adewole, and Yusupha Mboob for the main African parts. Dan was then a young actor from Manchester, 'Funmi a dancer from London, and Yusupha a Gambian master drummer. Horse & Bamboo regulars Nicky Fearn, Victoria Lee, Kathy Bradley and horse-handler Glen Wilson played the other roles. All members of the cast played music, along with MD Loz Kaye, so we also had a nice big procession band. The show was written and designed to be performed outdoors, and it toured very successfully in the UK, Ireland and the Netherlands.

Sam Ukala wrote:
"Like the African folk festival and story-telling theatres, whose aesthetics we drew on, Harvest of Ghosts deals with the past, present and future, the living and the dead. At the beginning of the play, Ancestors represent the dead, but at the end the living 'ghosts' of those killed for protesting injustice and inhumanity, living 'ghosts' such as the Ijo and Ogoni youths (who) are still fighting long after Ken Saro-Wiwa and hundreds more have been killed. The play suggests that the enemies of the people will be subdued by the combined efforts of the living and the dead. 'The Ogoni Troubles' may not end until the 'ghosts' overwhelm their harvesters and entrap them in their own destructive technology.

"The play is clearly moralistic and has the simple structure of a folk narrative as well as the intriguing compositeness and symbolism of the African festival. It focuses on serious political issues by delicately combining entertainment with public enlightenment in a language that cuts across educational backgrounds and national boundaries.

"In 1999, *Harvest of Ghosts* played to enthralled audiences who gave it robust praise. The Manchester Evening News of May 22 described it as a 'wordless wonder'…"

On his return to Nigeria, Professor Ukala revived Harvest of Ghosts as part of his new post at Delta State University, where he was Chairman of the Delta State Chapter of the Association of Nigerian Authors (ANA). His "Iredi War", a 'folk-script', won the 2014 Nigeria Prize for Literature, Africa's largest literary prize. It is based on the 1906 uprising of the Owa Kingdom (now part of Delta State) against oppressive British rule.

Sam Ukala died after a short illness in September 2021.

A Woodcut of 'Funmi Adewole in Harvest of Ghosts, 2023

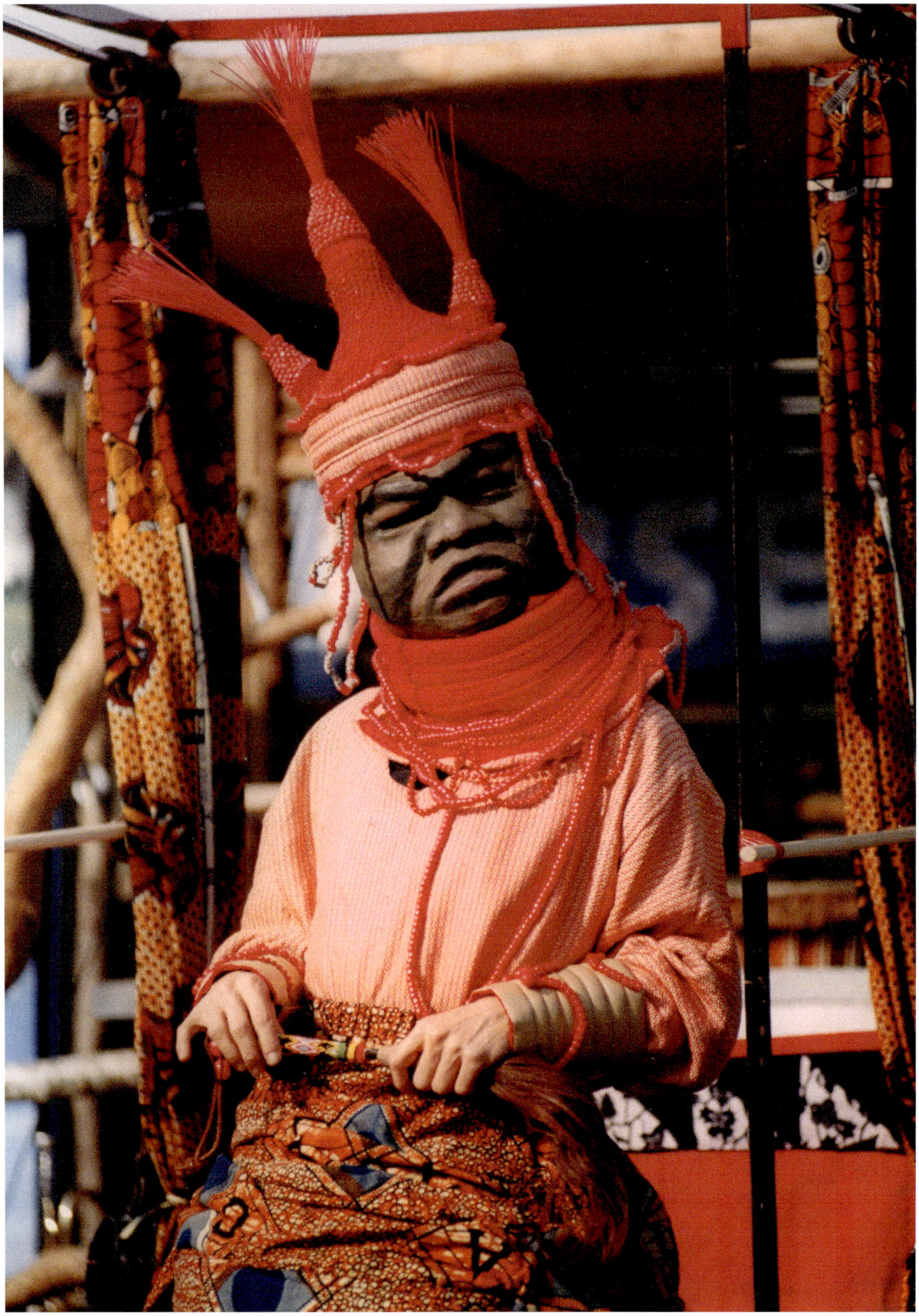

REVIEW:

"I was delighted to have the chance of seeing Horse + Bamboo once more, after a long interval, as they do not seem to have ventured to Greater Manchester for several years...I was also glad to see them performing outdoors, which is how their most distinctive and expert work began...

"Their highly evolved performances, being without dialogue but with constant live music and much use of masks, naturally gives themselves to universalism but the company is very ready to allow itself to be inspired by specific cultures far from its Rossendale base...

"It (Harvest of Ghosts) has taken various images of undisputed truth and, although they are closely related to particular historical events, and draw much of their power from this fact, have been wound into a picture of much more general import. Those...who saw these striking images and their lively performance to the accompaniment of the ever-involving music will have seen a powerful vision of how ruthless industrial development can destroy both natural and social health. The involvement of the audience was clear even when they were silent, made the clearer by sudden cries, such as "No! No!" when Kika handed the merchant back his gun, and by the rapturous applause at the end. The vivid masks helped to bind together the historical conflation...(and) though of African features, are of the style used by Horse + Bamboo in other works in other polities but they naturally fit into a culture where masks have played a leading part in the dramatic expression of religious and social belief, seen here in their own style on the ancestral spirits and around the shrine. Many divers talents and insights have gone into this work and they have been united in a great achievement."

Manchester Theatre Journal 1999

24. THE GIRL WHO CUT FLOWERS, 2000

In 1998 I received a postcard from Sandy Spieler, the Artistic Director of *In The Heart of the Beast*, a mask and puppet theatre based in Minneapolis. She wrote about a close friend of hers, an 'awesome maker' called Alison Duddle. After 5 years working with the US theatre company Alison was moving back to the UK with her husband. Sandy strongly recommended Alison to me, and suggested that I might like to meet with her.

Alison visited us later that year, and briefly helped on a *Guided Imagery* show. She also helped by making some of the puppets for *Harvest of Ghosts*. Alison was indeed a very good maker, with a natural sense of draughtsmanship and design, as well as being genuinely excited by and committed to mask and puppet theatre. Overall, she was an important addition to the company, and we got on well both personally and as work colleagues. It seemed inevitable that I would ask her to work more closely with me, leading to Alison helping me to develop the script of the next show, *The Girl Who Cut Flowers*. Alison directed one of the main sections of the show, which was inspired by the nursery rhyme drawings and paintings of the Portuguese artist Paula Rego.

The production was performed in a small and claustrophobic set, which was designed using a highly forced perspective. It was another strange and dark show, but despite this it turned out to be a very popular one. Alison made the majority of the female masks, and I made the male characters and the animals. Somehow that particular division of labour between us became our habit over the next decade.

The story starts with a dream-like parade of half-glimpsed nursery rhyme characters, and a giant hand places a large bundle in the dream-space. The bundle twitches and, very slowly, a young Girl emerges from it. She finds that she's trapped in the room, and after searching everywhere for a possible escape, she gives up in despair and curls up in the dark. Once she is asleep a grotesque Goat leans through a window into the room; the Goat steals her soul then leaves, disappearing into a dark Forest. When the Girl awakes she now finds that the door can be easily opened. She too sets off into the same Forest. The Goat re-appears throughout the story. One thing I really enjoyed was making each version of the Goat mask slightly less goat-like, and more human. Slowly and gradually the Goat turns into a handsome young man, and in his last iteration there are just two small stumps remaining on his forehead, the last traces of his horns.

We follow the Girl's escape and her journey from the room, her pursuit of the goat/man, moving from masked performance to puppetry, and then back again. This was the very last horse-drawn tour by the company, and even then it was a short one. Perhaps fittingly it took place in the very south of the Republic of Ireland.

Photographs from The Girl Who Cut Flowers, including the touring wagon.
Following pages: The Goat character from The Girl Who Cut Flowers

136

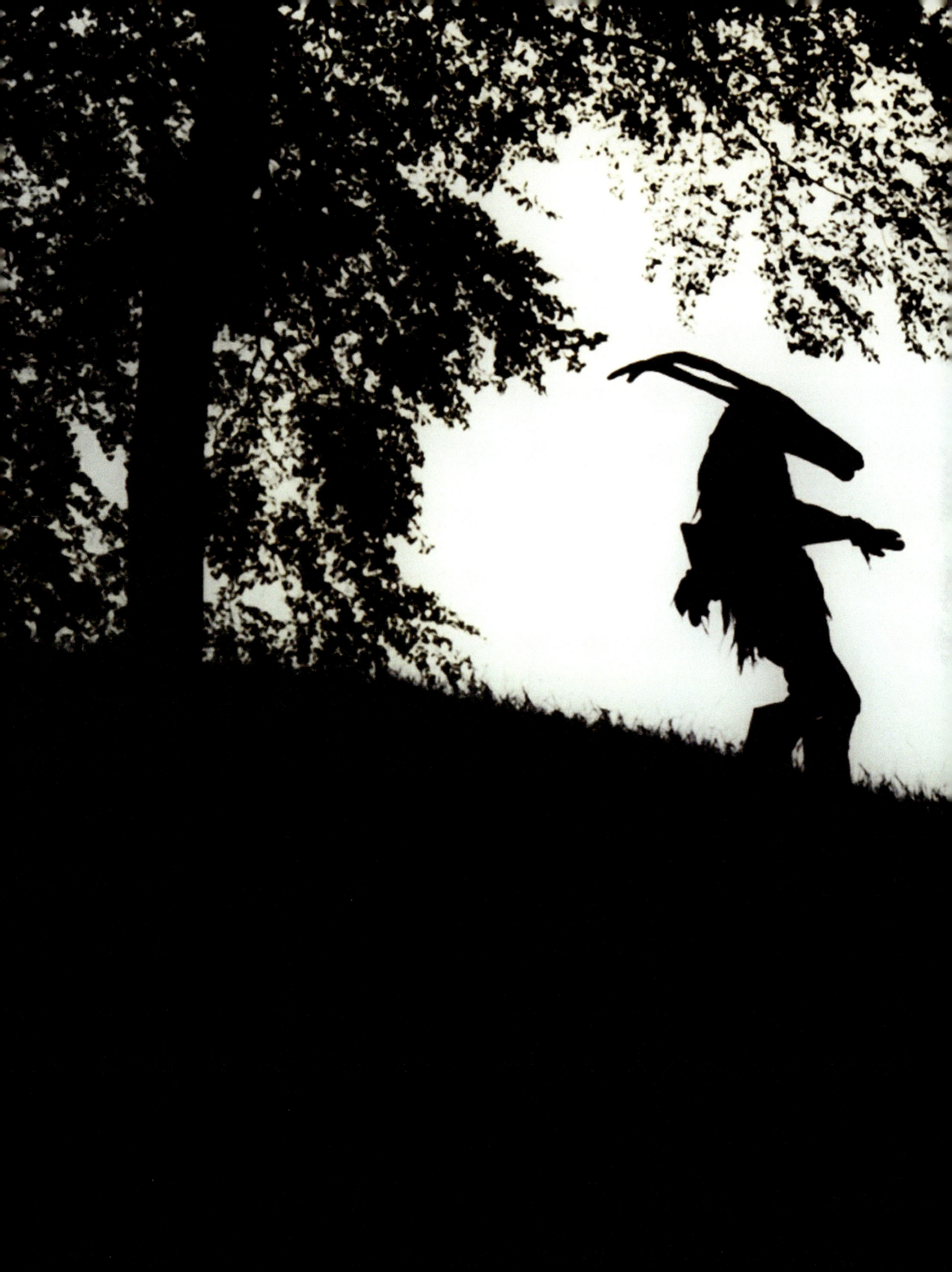

25. A PERIOD OF CHANGE

The period between 1998 and 2000 saw two major events that affected the company, either would have transformed the way we did things. Put together they meant a complete overhaul of many of our priorities and practices, and that in turn paved the way for still bigger changes in the future.

a) The end of Horse-drawn Touring

In 2000 Horse & Bamboo abandoned touring theatre shows using horse-drawn transport. There were a few things that came together to make this inevitable. First and foremost, the majority of our tours were paid for by local authorities. During the 1980s and early 1990s we would be contracted to tour to community venues such as village halls within one or more districts, for example within a county council area. There we would typically perform at three different venues each week. As a bonus the horse-drawn entourage would provide a colourful attraction that would be moving through the region – a day-long parade that people enjoyed. We also introduced ourselves at each new venue with a parade. But by the mid-1990s local authorities arts budgets were disappearing fast, and funding for the work simply dried up.

Second, the number of vehicles on British roads when we started horse-drawn touring in 1979 was about 17 million. By 2000, when we pulled the plug, it was 28 million (now it's over 40 million). Motorways had proliferated too, and travelling from A to B was often far from straightforward for horse-drawn vehicles. Police forces were not prepared, as they once had been, to provide us with an escort across busy major roads (there were usually one or two of these to be negotiated every summer). Put simply, it was getting far more dangerous. Motorists on country lanes no longer drove expecting a very slow moving convoy, 60 metres long, to be round the next corner. Near-misses were becoming more frequent, and I felt that sooner or later we would be involved in a serious accident.

Although horse-drawn touring was right at the heart of the company's work, and had a profound effect on our theatre practice, it was also true that most of our media coverage was focused on the way we travelled as a company. This was a source of frustration for me, and the one silver lining in abandoning our horses was that critics and reviewers were forced to take more notice of the theatre work itself, the stuff that ended up on stage. Whatever, in late summer 2000 our horses and wagons started a new life in the Scottish Borders, moving to the smallholding belonging to the last of our horse-handlers, Glen Wilson.

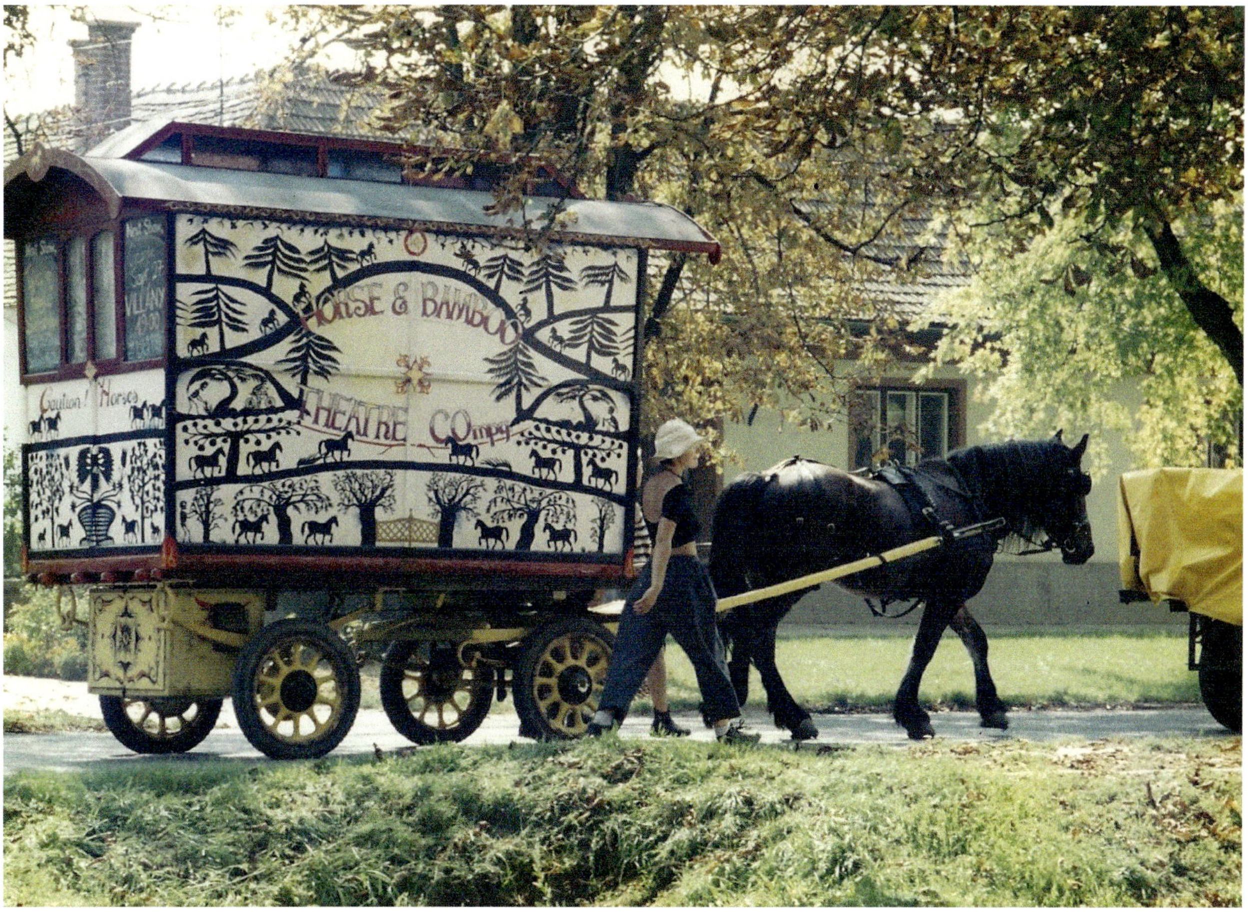
HORSE & BAMBOO
THEATRE COmpy
Caution! Horses
VILLANY

b) The Boo

By the mid-90s another source of frustration was that we had outgrown our base in Rawtenstall, which was both uncomfortable and not ideally equipped for theatre work (it had been a garage for large trucks), and especially for the rehearsal of shows. It was both cold and dirty, and impossible to heat. Our neighbour was needing to expand his furniture business and was offering us an extremely good price for the building, which we now owned. The main problem was that we had no time to look for an alternative home. Desperate to move things forward our neighbour went on a property hunt himself, and found an old Liberal Club that was for sale. It was just a few miles away, in Waterfoot, right in the heart of Rossendale, and he persuaded Sally Martin, our administrator, and myself to come along with him to check it out. Initially sceptical, I took one look and was immediately persuaded – the building was four or five times the size of the existing Rawtenstall space, and the main hall had a beautiful semi-sprung wooden floored hall – perfect for theatre, and with plenty of space for an audience. Better still, the price was actually lower than the one being offered for our current workshop.

So, the deed was done. We made the move in 1997, and raised money to fix the roof and convert what had been a slipper factory into an arts centre. The move meant that we suddenly found ourselves in a far more comfortable building, on the main road through the valley, and with a potential not only to house the Horse & Bamboo company, but to become an arts centre and a venue of our own, something which we had never had before. In most ways it was a dream come true, and something that other companies were envious of, especially as we owned the building ourselves – something almost unheard of in British theatre by the late 1990s.

Taking ownership of the Boo, which the building was soon known as (although it reverted back to Horse & Bamboo in 2022), sowed seeds that gradually, over the next few decades, began to create a potential source of conflict for the company. This was between Horse & Bamboo as an arts company that focused on creating its own original, highly visual theatre, and The Boo, a venue, a workshop and a community arts facility. But for the next few year, things developed in encouraging directions, and the two things operated effectively, side by side. During this period the company created some of its best and most successful productions.

Left: The Boo c.2006
Right: The Boo as an exhibition space - Beyond The Boundary 1999

26. COMPANY OF ANGELS, 2001-2004

Breakdown

One night, I think in 1999, while staying with the touring company in the Netherlands, in the beautiful village of Holysloot, I woke up and thought the ceiling was collapsing in on me; everything in the room was swirling around as if on a ship in a hurricane. I couldn't work out what was happening at all, but I knew it was something serious - not just a bad dream or the effects of food or drink. It was three in the morning but I just wanted to get home; in a panic I grabbed everything, woke up some of the company to let them know what was happening, and set off on the drive back to Rossendale.

"When I returned I went straight to the doctor, my mind was crazy with all sorts of thoughts. I suppose that it was a particularly pressurised time, partly because Sam Ukala, the Nigerian playwright, was coming to work (and live) with me. Perhaps part of it was worrying about how this would work out and if I was up to it, as Sam was a well-known published writer and the head of a University English Department. But in retrospect I think anxieties of all sorts had been creeping up on me over many years. I was diagnosed with depression and anxiety and put on antidepressant pills. For a week or so I was in a terrible state, and I must have put Kay through the wringer. Oddly I was able to hide most of it at work and, with just a few exceptions, I managed to continue to turn up and work in the Horse & Bamboo studios and carry on, almost as usual. I opened up about things to Alison, and she was an enormous help to me during this period. When I see photos of myself at the time I'm amazed at how normal I look, whereas inside I felt completely broken. It was in the lead up to the Millennium, and the company was committed to two large-scale projects. I didn't feel capable of leading them but Alison stepped in and valiantly took on the job of overseeing Manchester's Millennium Parade, which involved a large number of workshops with the city's diverse communities. She did this readily and effectively, and in the process rescued both the company's finances and my mental health.

Then slowly - perhaps because of the medication - things got a little better, even if anxiety still dogged me like a shadow. Over the next couple of years I went through a cycle of getting well enough to stop taking tablets; then my worries and depression would return until I went back on them. I was prescribed a course of CB therapy, which was OK but not, I think, especially effective. After going through this cycle three times I came to the conclusion I was going to be stuck in this way of living for ever and, of course, that was a big worry in itself.

One day I came across a book on mindfulness meditation while browsing in Waterstones. I've always tended to be sceptical about self-help, but something about this particular book felt right. I bought it, started reading, and began the 8-week course of meditation practice that it suggested. From the first session something clicked with me, and my spirits began to lift.

After those 8 weeks I sensed an improvement in my sense of myself, and how I saw the world around. In short, my inner strength slowly returned. I've never used antidepressant pills since. Generally (there are occasional lapses) I feel stronger all the time and now, every day, I take some time to meditate.

Company of Angels

Alison's role as assistant director was a sensible and natural development both for myself, especially at this stressful time, but it also worked for the company. The company's Board had wondered from time to time what it would do if and when I retired, or left for some reason, and having Alison as a natural successor was reassuring. By the time we got to making our next show, *Company of Angels*, we were sharing the writing, designing, making and directing. The original idea and outline had been inspired by a visit I made to an exhibition of paintings by Charlotte Salomon at the Royal Academy, but the production was very much a joint effort.

Salomon had been murdered in Auschwitz. Despite only being 26 she produced an amazing series of several hundred vivid gouaches telling the story of her life. Her visual story included the background to her immediate family; the growth of Nazism, and the series of events that led her to death in a concentration camp. These Charlotte planned to be bound together as *Life. Or Theatre?*. It was an ambitious and almost operatic concept which included some text along with suggestions for music alongside her paintings.

Despite the grimness of the subject, Salomon's work is full of life and colour, even humour. It's a remarkable testament, and to this day remains seriously under-appreciated. We worked with the Jewish Historical Museum in Amsterdam, who hold Salomon's complete collection. We paid them for copyright for some of the material, but they wouldn't allow any direct use of the images in our production. This forced us to re-imagine and re-make all aspects of her story. Although we decided to follow Charlotte Salomon's style closely, in some ways the limitations imposed by the Museum liberated us from copying things too slavishly. Again, it was a very successful show, and understandably generated a lot of interest from Jewish groups and Holocaust survivors. As a result many of the shows included an introduction (or post-show discussion) from survivors.

It also led to three tours of the USA in 2004. We used a new US cast, with the exception of Jonny Quick, a regular performer and maker with Horse & Bamboo, who had also been in the UK production. Alison's *In The Heart of the Beast* contacts in Minneapolis were invaluable, and she went back to the USA in order to redirect the show and the subsequent tours, including at a Puppeteers of America Festival.

REVIEWS:

A hypnotic theatre piece, rich with dream-like imagery. "Company of Angels" achieves a delicate balancing act. Salomon's story is undeniably sad but it also manages to highlight those moments where the artist experienced genuine happiness. ~ **Big Issue Review (UK)**

Thank you so much for your marvellous and creative performance...The whole show was amazing and spoke evocatively about Charlotte's paintings. Wonderful. ~ **Professor Lesley Ferris, Chair of Theater, Ohio State University**

[Company of Angels] is one of the most magic, sweet, profound and qualitative performances I've seen.... Combining the cruelty of the reality of a war, with the magic of the innocent world of a child, you spoke right to my heart.... It was so excellent, I almost forgot that the heads were masks! ~ **Nassia Choleva, Exeter University (UK)**

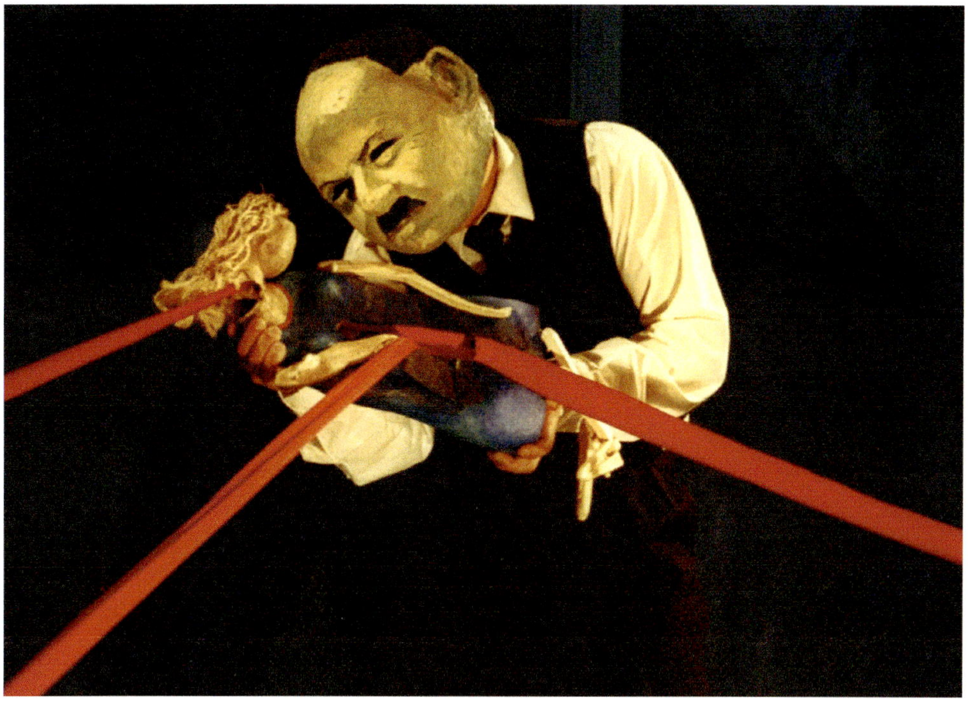

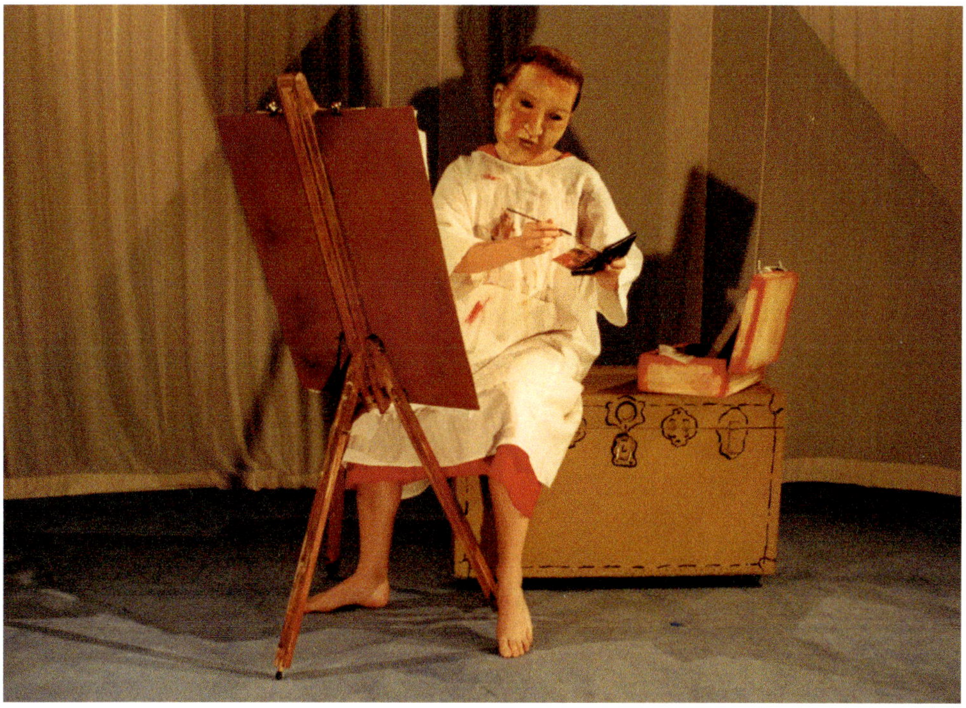

27. WORK FOR CHILDREN AND YOUNG PEOPLE

Horse & Bamboo were next approached about creating a children's Christmas show by Manchester's Royal Exchange Studio. We were keen on the idea and I wrote a script. Alison was interested in creating shows for young people and my script, *In The Shadow of Trees*, fitted the bill perfectly.

Alison directed, which was important for me as I was still in recovery from my depression, although I designed and made the set. We both contributed to the masks and puppets. Chris Davies wrote and played music, while the Exchange's Richard Owen devised an impressive lighting design.

This show was a huge success and at the end-of-year MEN awards it won in two categories, for the design and for the production. My stage design was included in an exhibition of contemporary stage designs at the Victoria & Albert museum. *In The Shadow of Trees* then went on to tour for two years.

Little Leap Forward

As Alison rapidly gained confidence as a director, it was becoming clear that her main interest was for children's stories. She was influenced by a number of excellent illustrated children's books, looking at the possibility of using them as a source of inspiration for her theatre work. Somehow during this time she hooked up with Barefoot Books. Barefoot was a publisher that concentrated on books for children, and Alison got into discussion with Tessa Strickland, Barefoot's founder. They were about to publish *Little Leap Forward*, which was a new venture for them as it was an autobiographical story for older children and adults. The author was Guo Yue, who had already achieved some fame as a Chinese classical bamboo flute virtuoso – and a chef.

We met with Yue and his wife Clare Farrow, who had translated the book, in late 2007 it was decided that Clare would work closely with Alison on the stage play. Meanwhile I would design and build the set for the touring production. Yue would also work closely with Loz Kaye, our Musical Director, on the music.

Yue contributed his own flute parts, which were central to the story. By now we were mainly touring without musicians, using recorded soundtracks as a way of cutting costs. Technical advances in sound equipment and recording had made this far more acceptable, although it was not a complete substitute for having live music, and whenever possible we would revive this practice.

For this production it was vital that we worked closely with Yue and Clare, but they were both constantly busy with other projects. It meant that the development of the show took considerably longer than previous H&B productions. Eventually the show opened at the Royal Exchange in Manchester, May 2009 and then toured into 2010.

Left: From In the Shadow of Trees, 2005
Above and following pages: From Little Leap Forward, 2009

REVIEW:

The Chinese flautist Guo Yue, whose name means Little Leap Forward, was eight when Mao Zedong declared the Cultural Revolution in 1966. Like many intellectuals, his school-teacher mother was declared a counter-revolutionary and sent to the country to be "re-educated" and dig mud out of the river.

Inspired by the children's book of the same name, but suitable for all ages, Horse & Bamboo's show – a ravishing, wordless mix of mask work, puppetry, shadow play and music – tells Guo Yue's story. It captures all the intensity of being eight: the brightness of the colours, the vividness of sound, the swooping shifts between exhilaration and sudden fear.

The story is linear, but this fleeting hour is so textured that the overall effect is impressionistic. The cut-out style paper design is just one of many visual pleasures: Mao's marching Red Army is depicted by tiny puppets springing out of the kitchen drawers; the perspective is constantly shifting – one minute you feel as if you are looking down on red fish swimming up a river, the next you are watching a tiny puppet bird crossing the wide sky. The song bird, captured and caged, becomes a metaphor for Guo Yue himself, his lost mother and for the music career that eventually leads him leave China. The violence of the Cultural Revolution is never shirked.

The piece is full of grace and simple beauty – if it has a fault, it is that the storytelling is sometimes a little unclear, and it is not always easy to work out who all the characters are: it's worth reading the programme beforehand. But this is a lovely, maverick show that focuses on ordinary lives overtaken and trampled by history.

Little Leap Forward **** By Lyn Gardner, The Guardian 2009

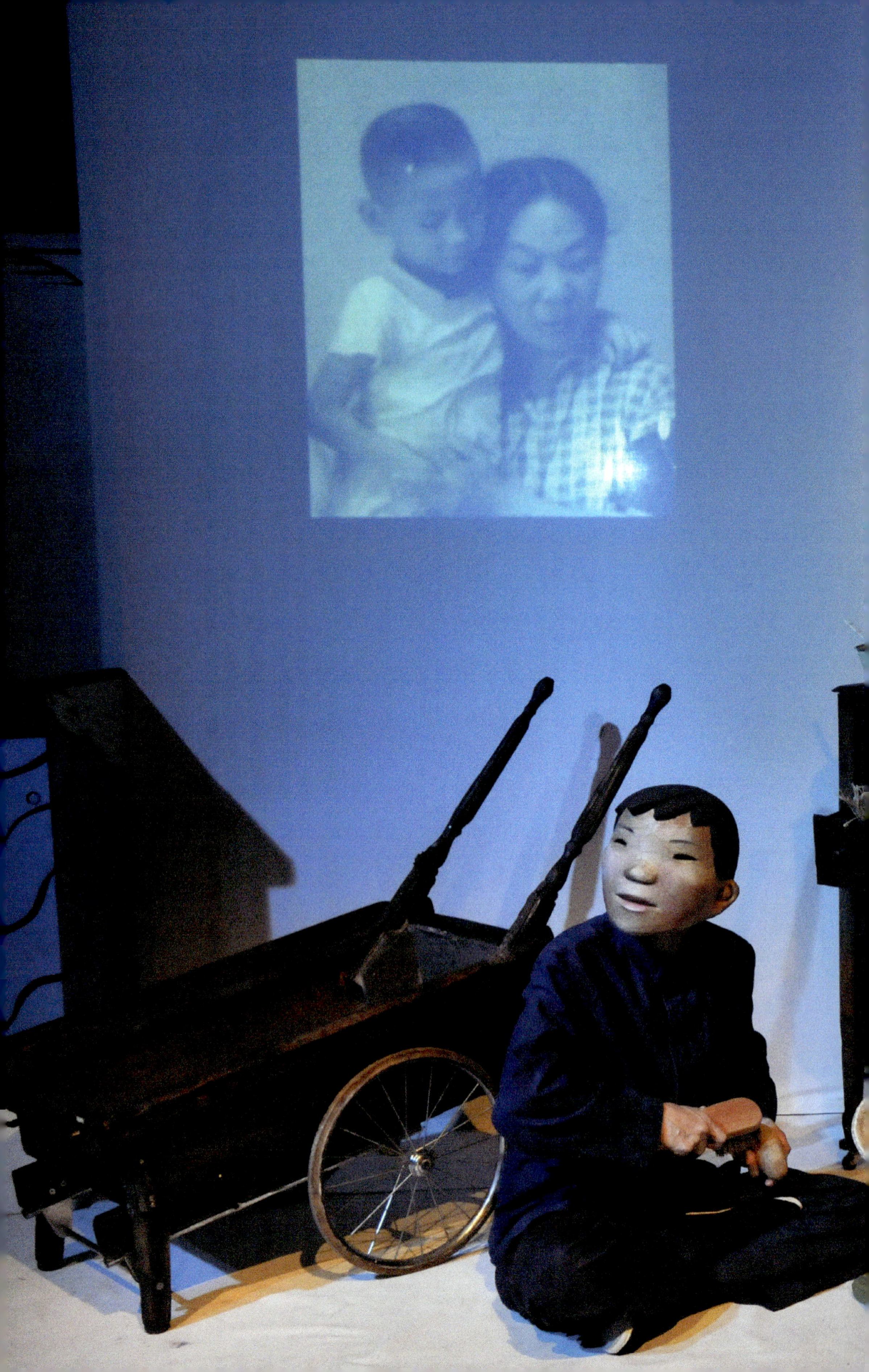

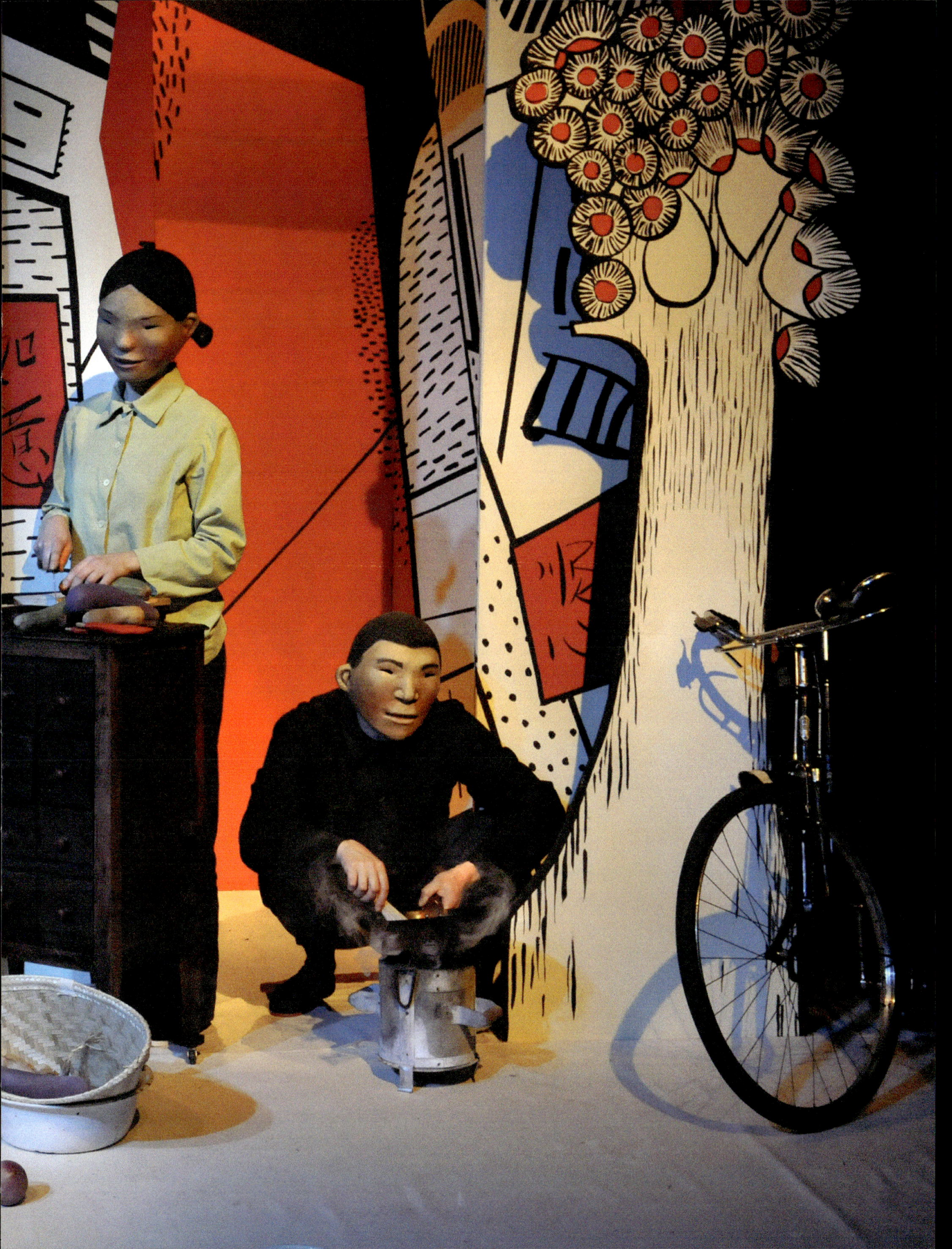

28. STOCKTAKE 1

Thirty years after I had formed Horse & Bamboo the company had expanded to a point where we had two Artistic Directors and owned a building large enough to provide us with a workshop as well as a successful community venue for arts events. Alison was by now working almost independently from me within the company. She had successfully developed the Boo space both as a venue and a place where she could pursue her interest in children's theatre. That all seemed like good news to me. It meant that we had a successor Artistic Director in place and it gave me the freedom to continue to experiment with my own theatre work.

When I began working with Alison I considered myself as a director of visual theatre, a way of working that developed from my background as a visual artist. Now, Alison's growing interest in puppetry was introducing me to a world of puppeteers and puppet companies. Puppetry had its own language, traditions and shorthand; its own raft of technical skills, fixes, and aesthetics. I had always used puppets, true, but in my mind they were all of a one with masks, painted sets, and other objects used in a performance, primarily there to tell a story. But now, increasingly, performers were joining the company as puppeteers, specialists and skilled practicioners in exactly the same way as a musician might be.

Several times during this period I visited the impressive international puppet festival at Charleville-Meziers, and saw some of the hugely varied work, both good and not-so-good, being done by puppeteers and puppet companies. This naturally rubbed off on me; at the same time I began to notice Horse & Bamboo itself sometimes being described as a 'puppet company'. Nevertheless I continued to see myself as a director of visual theatre – a theatre that included and contained puppetry in the same way that it included music, masks, and performing objects.

From 2011 until 2016 Alison continued working on theatre for children and young people. Some of the shows, like *Red Riding Hood* (2011) I worked on with her; others like *The Nightingale*, I had almost no involvement in. However she had an extremely supportive team of puppeteer/performers including Mark Whitaker, Jonny Quick and Aya Nakamura.

Left: Red Riding Hood
Top: Moominland Midwinter

Alison also achieved one of her dreams during this period, which was to co-direct a successful medium-scale production of one of Tove Jansson's *Moomintroll* stories, which we had both loved and toyed with as a potential project for many years. It wasn't an easy or straightforward process, but eventually Alison was able to co-direct *Moominland Midwinter* in conjunction with *the egg*, in Bath, and the resulting production was well received.

This situation might have gone on developing, with Alison directing Horse & Bamboo productions aimed at younger audiences, along with the annual puppet festival, which brought national and international companies to The Boo for an exciting week or more of workshops and productions. But the company had been gradually transforming into a very different beast from what it had been 15 years earlier.

Horse & Bamboo was now one of the highest funded arts organisations in Lancashire. We were an NPO (National Portfolio Organisation), which meant that the company was considered 'strategically important', and its funding was guaranteed in blocks of three years, which provided an increased level of financial security. Along with this, however, the company was expected to commit itself to the Arts Council's priorities in a whole range of areas, such as the type of audiences that it 'targeted' through to how the company marketed itself. These guidelines were increasingly insisted upon, and it was the Horse & Bamboo Board who were now ultimately responsible for all of the managerial decisions taken by the company. We had a senior manager and a team of office-based staff who looked after the finances, marketing and so on, and it was frowned on for the artists to become too involved in this type of decision making. Naturally all of this began to change the way that we did things. It didn't happen overnight, but the changes came slowly but surely, especially after 2000. On the surface Horse & Bamboo was able to continue just as we always had done, and I still continued to be seen as the overall director of the company, although eventually I shared this role with a Chief Executive. Nationally, even this degree of power for an artistic director of a theatre company was unusual within the funded arts by 2015.

29. VEIL 2008

From 2001 on it was impossible not to be aware of many issues relating to the Middle East and the wider Muslim world. The news media were in overdrive about it, though most of what was being written was clearly poorly informed.

Meanwhile, the Horse & Bamboo Board, encouraged by the Arts Council, were taking on more trustees from a business background. From the Board came an ambition to increase the scale of our productions. This was in the belief that by doing so Horse & Bamboo would be seen as increasingly professional and business-like by funders, both in the private and in the public sectors. This went hand-in-hand with taking on business advisors, marketing specialists and consultants. These arts professionals, with a circular logic, further encouraged the ambition of the Board. A successful one-off grant of £78,000 from the Arts Council for the production must have made them feel that they were heading in the right direction.

So *Veil* grew out of an intersection of two things – my interest in the issues associated with the Islamic world, and an Arts Council inspired momentum to professionalise, whatever that meant. The first part was fascinating to me, and I began to research the politics, history, and culture of the Middle East, particularly the Arab world. I wanted to find out as much as I could about these things. I met and talked with my good friends Parminder Kaur and Halima Cassell about their views and experiences. The issue of women wearing the burhka was very much in the news at this time, and Parminder introduced me to a number of her young women friends to talk about this and other related issues, and especially about the choices they were making in their own lives.

I saw that veils came in all forms. Colonial history was a shady business, and in any case it was hugely misrepresented and misunderstood in the West. The plunder of the historic sites in the Middle East, which commenced in Napoleonic times, continued right through the world wars. The post-war 'settlements' that divided the Arab world into its current borders were decided largely in order to maintain western spheres of interest. The lure of enormous oil-based wealth was obviously the main determinant in more recent interventions. The scarves and burkhas worn by some of the women were almost the smallest part of it, although it was the issue that appeared to most obsess the press and media.

152

As a result of the Horse & Bamboo Board's determination to make a show that was capable of touring to larger venues I was given the opportunity to plan things on a grander scale than I had been able to since the 1990s. We had mixed fortunes in casting, but managed to contract Nabil Musa, an Iraqi Kurd, as a performer and advisor, and I had the support of an Iraqi artist, Faliha Kadhim, who had fled Baghdad a few years earlier, to help with the production.

I was pleased with my script, which brought together personal and historical stories in a broad sweep, moving through time from the ancient Kingdom of Babylon to present day London. I wanted to show that non-verbal, visual theatre was capable of creating large-scale, epic, tightly woven narratives. The story was a powerful one, and ambitious. It involved a rape, an ancient curse, dreams, the current military occupation of Iraq, and an archaeological dig in Nineveh. The emotional thrust was the search by twin sisters, separated at birth, to each rediscover their twin. The cast were excellent, Loz Kaye's music was brilliant, the set by Katherina Radeva beautifully effective, and Richard Owen's lighting and the film work by Erik Knudsen were fabulous.

However, the Board's financial hopes for the production were not to be realised. It proved difficult to sell to venues at the level that we needed to cover our costs. We had a reasonable opening run at the Lawrence Batley in Huddersfield, and a brilliant sell-out show at The Lowry, where it looked superb. Otherwise the tour was rather stunted, and it didn't attain the optimistic targets that our Producer, Board and the various consultants were hoping for. Then, in September 2008 came the financial crash, and the hope of another more financially lucrative tour of *Veil* in 2009 and beyond, were dashed.

REVIEW:

Veil, Brighton Corn Exchange, Brighton, April 18. Paul Smith

Veil is not only an evocative and haunting work but, unlike much visual theatre, presents a multilayered narrative full of depth and nuance. The central characters are twin sisters separated at birth and brought up in different cultures. The girls are born to an Iraqi woman raped by a Western archaeologist, who then steals one of the babies and returns home, along with the treasures he has removed from the desert.

The human story is a reflection of wider themes; of the pillaging of the country's past, the influence of culture and the current conflict. The girls' nightmares and sense of loss and separation seem to be a metaphor for the fears and mistrust separating East and West. The production itself is also multilayered. The narrative is played out using voices and visuals, puppetry and lighting, music mime and masks. The masks are a veil across the characters' emotions and yet feelings are conveyed through body shape and gesture; through Loz Kaye's mournful, lamenting score; and by a beautifully lit set which evokes the eye-blinking glare of the desert.

In the second half, the families' fragmented story moves west. The girls, now grown women, eventually are reunited at an exhibition of the ageing archaeologist's treasures. Again the secrets and lies of family life being echoed in wider conflicts of culture and identity. This is Horse and Bamboo's 30th anniversary production and is a beautiful exposition of their visually arresting theatre. It is complex, but works wonderfully well on many levels, asking questions but allowing the audience to delve behind the veil as deeply as they want to.

*

Within a few years it had become painfully obvious that the days of touring our own productions, certainly in the sense that we had been doing since 1979, were drawing to a close. *Veil's* short life turned out to be a harbinger of this. It was particularly poignant given both the quality of the show, and the aspirations that the Horse & Bamboo Board had for the production in hoping that it might kickstart a new and ambitious chapter in the company's touring work. Ultimately perhaps the desire to professionalise just didn't marry too well with the soul of the company.

Ian Tilton Photographer
www.iantilton.net

155

30. DEEP TIME CABARET 2011

After *Veil* I was in a kind of limbo. I had been delighted with the show and wasn't sure how I could better it, especially now that budgets had suddenly been reduced again. In terms of the forms of visual and physical theatre that we had developed over the years, it seemed we had, for now anyway, exhausted them – and I didn't want to go on repeating myself.

I had been directing a part of a local project called *Valley of Stone*, about the quarrying heritage of the Rossendale Valley. *Valley of Stone* was organised by Rossendale Groundwork, sympathetically managed by Liz Hinchcliffe, and well funded by the Heritage Lottery Fund. One thing I enjoyed was that it enabled me to work with other visual artists and film-makers. It also revived my interest in geology and the concept of Deep Time (sometimes called Geological Time - a measuring of time in millions, and even billions, of years). The project was multi-faceted, and it provided an opportunity to try a new approach to putting together a theatre production.

The artist Tracey Holland had worked on *Valley of Stone*, where she made a short film about the geology of Rossendale. I decided to use this as a starting point; a kind of touchstone for a performance. So I wrote a freewheeling play drawing intuitively on all sorts of sources. Folk stories, myths, astronomy, and with a quirky but pedagogical slant to it. Another influence was a young Anglo-Chinese animator, Steff Lee, who was recommended to us through a contact of Alisons. From the beginning Steff possessed an uncanny ability to read my mind and put it onto film.

I also tried experimental production techniques. We used wind-up lights on stage, projecting live camera feed, and bringing the backstage to the front stage, so changing costumes and masks were not hidden from the audience. Mostly I tore up the Horse & Bamboo how-to-do-it manual and started the process of creating theatre afresh.

Rather wonderfully we were able to perform Deep Time Cabaret deep underground, in the Clearwell Caves complex in the Forest of Dean. It was the perfect space for the show. The stage and all the props had to be carried by hand down to the large cavern in which we set up the stage and performed.

The production wasn't to everyone's liking. At one show someone wrote in the Comments Book 'What have you done with Horse & Bamboo?'. But to others *Deep Time Cabaret* was refreshing and stimulating. For me it shook things around enough to forget the financial disappointment of the *Veil* tour. It also gave me the space and the opportunity to find a new approach to making theatre.

Above: Deep Time Cabaret set in Clearwell Caves, Forest of Dean

158

REVIEW:

The Guardian: Horse & Bamboo Theatre – Deep Time Cabaret, Rosemary Branch Theatre, London Suspense London Puppetry Festival, 6 November 2009. Reviewed by Matthew Isaac Cohen

Punch and Judy struggle over a slapstick at the centre of a twirling galaxy while Stephen Hawking's mechanical voice asks, 'Why are we here? Where did we come from?' Mummers festooned in cloth. An old union of mineworkers' song, sung with gusto. A film by Tracey Holland about the Rossendale Hills. A recounting of the Greek myth of the origin of the Milky Way, with paper figures animated in real-time and projected onto a screen. Swinging light bulbs and a constructivist set. Images of medieval agriculture.

Deep Time Cabaret is a mash-up of folk tradition and emergent technology, old questions and new problems, a profound meditation on current ecological imbalances, and an applied theatre project. The 'deep time' in the title refers to geological time, which operates on an entirely different scale to human time. From the perspective of deep time, Greek myth, Stephen Hawking, and all of human history are part of the same moment. Our scamperings across the planet's surface are of trivial significance, but the damage our industries have wrought is consequential, though perhaps still reversible. The problem is our lack of attention to and appreciation for the world around us. Quoting American poet Ralph Waldo Emerson, a narrator intones: 'If the stars should appear but one night every thousand years how man would marvel and stare.'

Horse & Bamboo encourage their audience to marvel and stare, not only at the rare spectacle they have compiled, which is both responsive to their own ecological position and universal in ambition, but more importantly at the universe outside the performance. The work is abstractly poetic, but also entertaining, with a narrative enacted by hand puppets at the work's core. A Punch-like figure, dressed in white with a turban wrapped around his head, mines the heart of the earth and takes it back to his domicile, storing it in a coffin-like container. The heart transforms into a woman, who shortly expires. Punch then restores her to her proper place in the bowels of the earth. Punch is deftly swazzled and while I would have preferred to have seen Punch's anarchic streak on greater display (his functionality reminding me of American WPA Punch and Judy shows which cast Punch as a traffic warden), I admit I am a sucker for Old Red Nose, and appreciate every attempt at updating and re-contextualising him. Others, perhaps, will have similar reactions to other aspects of this richly intertextual production. The performance implicates the audience. It makes us more than witnesses to environmental degradation. We are 'here' not only to enjoy Punch's antics, but for something more. We have been hailed. What we do now is up to us.

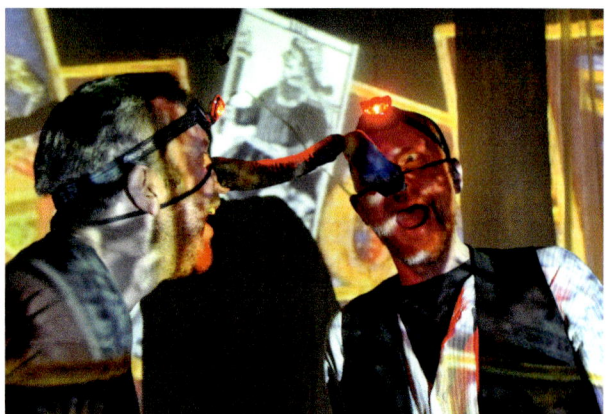

31. ANGUS, WEAVER OF GRASS, 2012/13

By 2011 the Arts Council's priority was funding the development of our base, the Boo, as a venue and Horse & Bamboo as a community arts company. It looked like the end of our touring work.

The cavalry came in the shape of Creative Scotland, which was now entirely separate from the Arts Council of England. Horse & Bamboo had built a strong following in Scotland, and we had toured there many times. It just so happened that I was hoping to create a show around the character of Angus McPhee, who I had heard of from my friend Chris Spears. Chris lived on Berneray, and we had first met in 1984 during the planning of our Seol tour of the Outer Hebrides.

Angus McPhee

Angus McPhee left South Uist in 1914 to fight in the Great War, but was soon invalided out. He then spent half a century in a Highland asylum as an elective mute, choosing not to speak. Instead, he wove fanciful clothing from the grasses and other vegetation that he harvested from the hospital farm. Then, in 1994, Angus was suddenly returned to Uist as part of the Care in the Community scheme. Towards the end of his life he began to receive wider attention as a significant Outsider Artist. Angus died in 1997.

Chris wasn't the only person with a connection to Horse & Bamboo who knew of Angus. Another was Joyce Laing, the Director of Pittenweem Festival. Joyce had been asked to vouch for us during the controversy around the *Needles in a Candleflame* show in 1983. She had also written a small book outlining Angus's story that Chris had posted to me. It was Joyce who had 'discovered' Angus during his long stay in Craig Dunain Psychiatric Hospital in Inverness. She then publicised his extraordinary work so it became more widely known. Joyce had also visited Angus in his last years back with his family in Iochdar on South Uist. She found that he was now talking a little, and was able to interview him.

I went to visit Joyce at her museum and gallery of *Art Extraordinary* in Pittenweem. This collection held most of Angus's existent work, and we talked about old times – and about Angus. Eventually I went to the islands to meet with Angus's family – his grandchildren, nephews and nieces. They were polite and welcoming, but clearly a little dubious about my plan to write and then tour a play about their grandfather. This wasn't really surprising, as until recently Angus was hardly known, even to them. Now, all of a sudden he had reappeared, transported from a distant psychiatric unit. To top it all, he had become a sort of artistic celebrity.

Meanwhile, Esther Ferry-Kennington, our Producer, had done a great job in raising interest in Scotland about the idea of a show about Angus. The interest was also for a production that would be partly told in Gaelic. When it became clear that Creative Scotland would offer us financial support for this, the way was clear for me to further develop the idea.

Joanne B. Kaar

I immediately had a stroke of luck. Searching the internet I came across the work of Joanne B. Kaar. Joanne is a very talented weaver/artist living in Dunnet, Caithness, at the very northern tip of Scotland, further north than John O'Groats even. She had already created a few pieces of work in tribute to Angus McPhee, and so I made contact with her. The first enquiry ended in her Junk Mail box, and I briefly wondered if she wasn't going to be interested. But before long I found myself travelling up to pay a visit to her home and workshop. Joanne's work is extraordinary and an inspiration in itself, and Joanne and her husband Joe were extremely welcoming. I spent a couple of days talking about my ideas for a show about Angus's life. Once I clarified what I wanted she immediately signed up to recreating versions of Angus's weavings. Before long Joanne joined a group from Horse & Bamboo on a research and development week on Berneray. It was on this trip that I first met Angus's family.

Sealladh as boidhche na chunna sibhse riamh? Aonghas Mac-a-Phi a' fighe le feur.

Uncovering the secret

In fact Joanne's work on the weavings went far further than I had hoped for. She managed to discover exactly how he had managed to create his woven grass work. Until Joanne's work on this no-one knew exactly how Angus had made the woven grass costumes. Joanne's discoveries and her work for Horse & Bamboo led to her being commissioned first by Joyce Laing, and then by Scottish Museums, to replicate Angus McPhee's signature pieces. These replica weavings are now in the Scottish national collection. Joyce Laing also commissioned Joanne to recreate Angus's work for her *Art Extraordinary* collection.

Shortly after visiting Joyce I went with Loz Kaye to Glasgow to audition Gaelic singers for the production. We saw and heard six singers and instrumentalists. Each one was impressive, and it appeared that we were going to have to make a difficult choice. The last audition was with Mairi Morrison, a Lewis born singer and actor who was already well known in Scotland. The idea was to tell Angus's story in our usual way, using imagery and music, but with this show we would use traditional Gaelic songs. Mairi was the perfect person to help us with this. Not only was she a native Gaelic speaker, but she had a deep knowledge of traditional song, so Mairi was able to work with Loz on the whole musical context for the show. As things developed we began to introduce some spoken Gaelic in addition to the songs.

We were helped massively by Brian Ó hEadhra of the Bòrd na Gàidhlig, Scotland's national Gaelic language body. Also by Ceòlas, a Uist-based music organisation and An Lanntair, the gallery and arts centre in North Uist. As a result Esther was able to put together a tour of the Outer Hebrides.

The show opened at Iochdar, close to where Angus McPhee was born and died. His extended family came to the first show. They remembered my earlier visit and we spoke briefly before the show. Once again they were polite but reserved in a way I had found to be typical of most islanders. Throughout the performance I was nervous, wondering what the family would make of it. At the end Angus's nephew Iain came right over, grinning broadly. He congratulated me and it was clear that the show had met the family's approval. Other members of the family gathered around, happy with the outcome. This was the first and biggest hurdle, and we had cleared it.

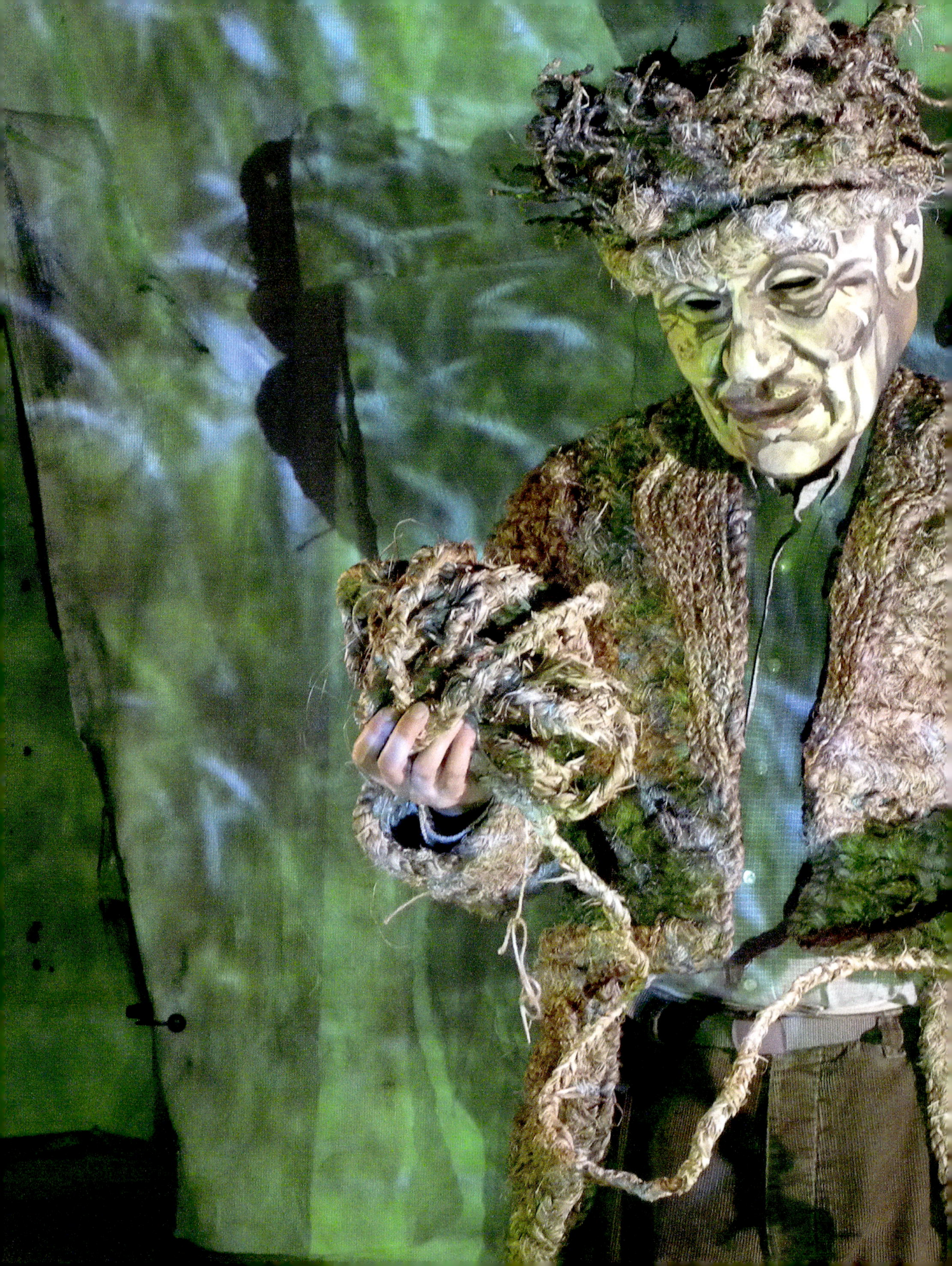

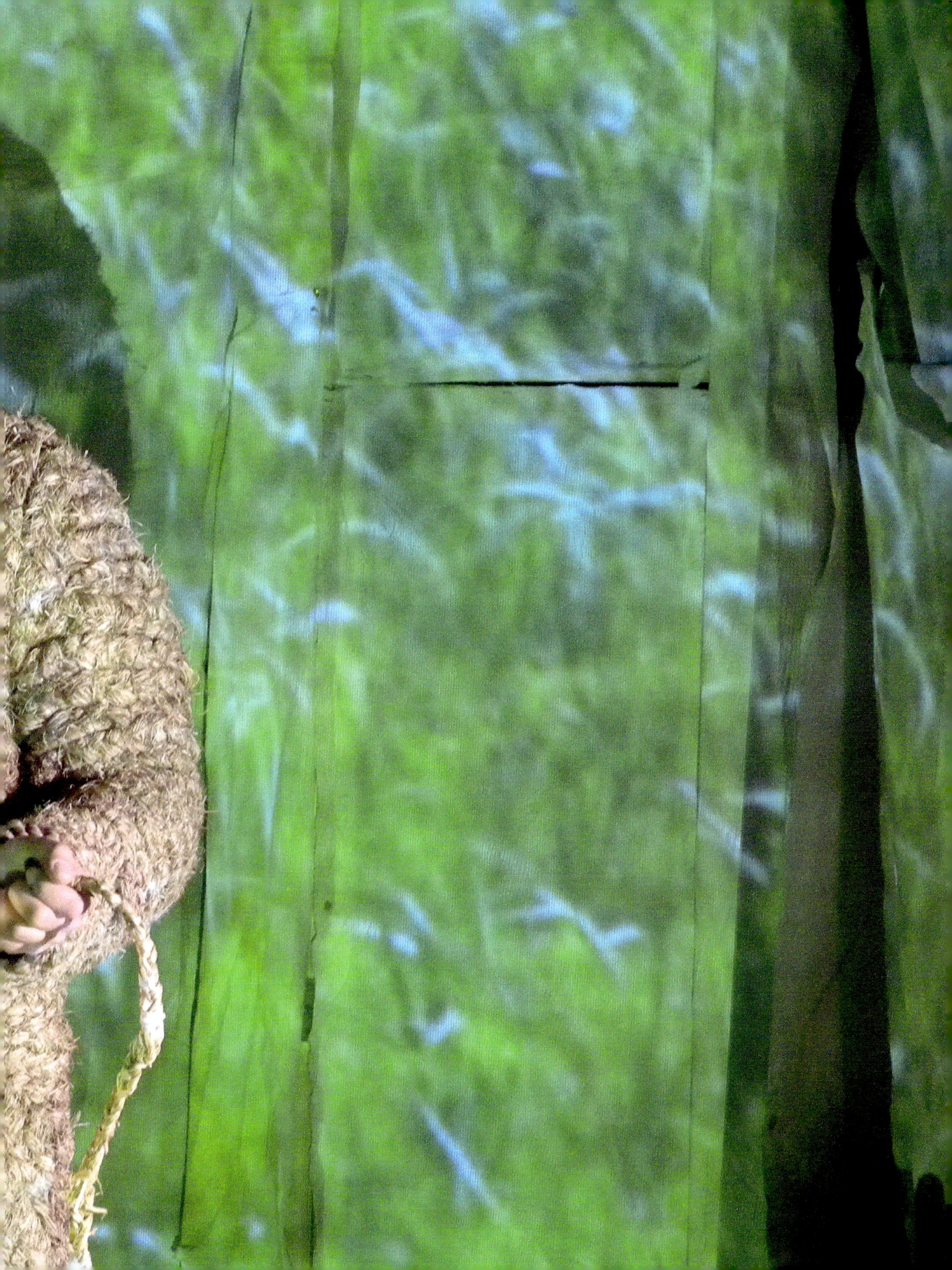

After that the tour went from strength to strength. It was showing to large and appreciative audiences everywhere it went. The publicity it created for the Gaelic language was important too. There was, of course, an irony in it being an English company (albeit with a strongly Scots cast) that had created a successful show with Gaelic the predominant language.

It was clear that Creative Scotland would be happy to support a second tour the following year. As word of the production spread we were also getting interest from English venues. These enquiries were usually because the production dealt with issues around mental health, rather than the language it was told in.

In 2013 it was noticeable how much things had changed. The name Angus McPhee seemed far better known throughout Scotland. This wasn't by any means simply the result of our show. A book had been published about Angus by the popular writer Roger Hutchinson. It was entitled *The Silent Weaver* and received a lot of publicity in Scotland. Roger had generously helped me during the writing of the script, sending me a draft of his book. He then went on to accompany some of our performances, giving an introduction and sometimes a question and answer session. I also met Donny Munro from Runrig, who had written a song (Weaver of Grass) about Angus some years before. Suddenly it was hard to escape the story of the Silent Weaver! On the North-East coast there was a festival based at several centres and hospitals to look more openly at mental health. The story of Angus – and our show – featured prominently in its programming.

Unfortunately Mairi had other commitments and couldn't make a second tour in 2013. I was worried that we wouldn't find a replacement singer and actor of her standard. Mairi spread the word and promised to help us audition. However our relief at finding a replacement for Mairi was short-lived. Our chosen candidate (Debbie Mackay) was snaffled by Alba TV to be a leading lady of its new Gaelic soap, *Bannan*. This all happened just two weeks before our rehearsal started. At the time the tour plans were thrown into total disarray, but with hindsight it was understandable that Debbie made the choice she did. Especially given the subsequent huge success of *Bannan*. In any case we contacted M.J. Deans who at short notice, and having been previously turned down by us for Debbie, stepped in. What a find she was! M.J turned out to be the perfect replacement for Mairi. Jordanna O'Neill replaced Frances Merriman, although we retained Jonny Quick and Mark Whitaker. Despite losing Debbie, in the end the second tour turned out to be every bit as successful as the first.

Angus – Weaver of Grass seemed to presage a revival of Gaelic language theatre in Scotland. How much it was part of that change is impossible to know. It was a great show that we were all very proud of. If it contributed in any way to create a climate that made the idea seem like a good one, then it was yet another reason to celebrate it.

REVIEW:
Angus – Weaver of Grass: review Northings website 2012

If you see one piece of theatre this year, see this. It is a compassionate performance, telling the life story of Angus McPhee, who was born and died on South Uist, but in between suffered the worst that British society could offer to a person with mental health problems. But this is not just a story about suffering, it's about dignity and the healing power of art. The play, created by Bob Frith and the Horse & Bamboo Theatre, mixes human actors and puppetry in a completely original way. Actors wearing masks interact with puppets, shifting seamlessly from character to puppeteer and back. A clever set, superb lighting and soundtrack, plus use of film and animation, and a combination of Gaelic and English words and songs, make this a many layered and fascinating experience.

It sounds complex, and it is, but it's far from difficult. The performances are witty and moving and the story is utterly compelling. After a happy rural Hebridean childhood, Angus became a soldier during the Second World War, during which he developed schizophrenia. He was incarcerated for 50 years in Craig Dunain hospital in Inverness, but for most of that time he didn't require drugs and, in a more enlightened era, would probably not have been in hospital at all. The delusions Angus experienced first as a soldier and then as he became more ill are brought vividly to the stage in a mix of movement, war footage, animation, puppetry, light and sound. The formal treatments meted out by the hospital included electro-convulsive therapy, and the scenes in the play where this is shown are among its most powerful.

Fortunately Angus found his own therapy on the hospital farm, where he wove grass, using techniques he had watched as a child for practical things like halters for horses. He created all sorts of grass objects: hats, bags and even giant boots, gloves, coats and suits, which he would hang on trees or hide under bushes. They were often burnt by hospital staff along with dead leaves, until eventually they were recognised as the artworks they clearly were. The reproductions of these objects, made for the play by Caithness-based textile artist Joanne B Kaar, are quite extraordinary. My only criticism of the play is that the long passage of years as Angus developed his mastery of grass was rather too swiftly played out. I wished that there had been more time spent exploring this craftwork, and the healing that it brought.

Throughout his long hospitalisation, Angus did not speak, and the play reflects this through a minimal use of voice, restricted to songs and a few brief bursts of narration. Mairi Morrison's singing is superb – unfussy, clear and heartfelt – and the blend of rich Gaelic and a pared-down sufficiency of English is original and very evocative. Altogether, this is the best piece of theatre I have seen in a long time. Catch it if you can. There is an accompanying exhibition about mental health, which adds yet another dimension to this really important and creative enterprise.

32. STOCKTAKE 2

By 2015 the Arts Council were looking to make funding cuts, while increasing their demands as to exactly what their clients priorities should, must, be. It was made clear that any grant support from the Arts Council was to be used for our building and community programming. It was not, we were told, to be used to write, create and produce further touring shows. The Arts Council were intransigent about this, and our Board and most of our office-based staff felt that they had no choice but to agree with them.

The most significant and dramatic decision taken during this period of upheavals happened suddenly at the end of 2016. It was decided by the Board to cut Alison Duddle's post as Joint Artistic Director. This came as an enormous shock to Alison, to me and to most of the artists in the company. Overnight it totally changed the direction and feel of Horse & Bamboo. I was approaching 70, and decided that I should now wrap things up in as tidy a way as possible, and retire from the company. From then on Horse & Bamboo would be run by an Executive Director.

It was a very painful time. One member of the Board resigned in protest. Inevitably Alison was devastated by the decision, and she fought it with the support of her Union, ultimately receiving a financial settlement. She now directs a new company, *A Bird In the Hand Theatre*, where she creates original shows and events, mainly for children, young people and in community settings. Several of Horse & Bamboo's regular performers, including Mark and Jonny, left with her, and they now frequently work with Alison and her new company.

Above: Woodcut, The Maskmaker (Alison Duddle) 2023
Left: Woodcut based on Alison's puppets from The Nightingale, 2023

33. DIFFERENT MOONS

Alison had been forced to leave the company, and its main focus now was changing from writing, creating and touring shows (Horse & Bamboo) to that of a venue with a community programme (The Boo). This seemed like a good time for me to move on. However, there was one thing that I still really wanted to do. That was to develop creative links with the local communities in East Lancashire from a South Asian background. This project became *Different Moons*.

HORSE + BAMBOO DIFFERENT MOONS

I discovered that there was no information on the history and background of the East Lancashire South Asian communities in the local libraries. Nothing even regarding such basic information as to how and why these communities had come to settle in the area. The central history library in Accrington contained one item. It was a thoughtful booklet produced by a local authority officer to help others understand some of the problems they might face when dealing with local South Asian communities, but it was many years out of date..

I decided that what was needed was a new approach, which should begin by interviewing some of the first immigrants to record their stories. I wanted to do this with care and publish the results in book form so that the libraries would finally have some substantive background documentation. After all, people of South Asian heritage now make up a large part of the Rossendale community. From the beginning I also wanted this to be the starting point for an extended project. It needed to avoid the fate of previous schemes which had achieved their immediate ends, but had then disappeared.

170

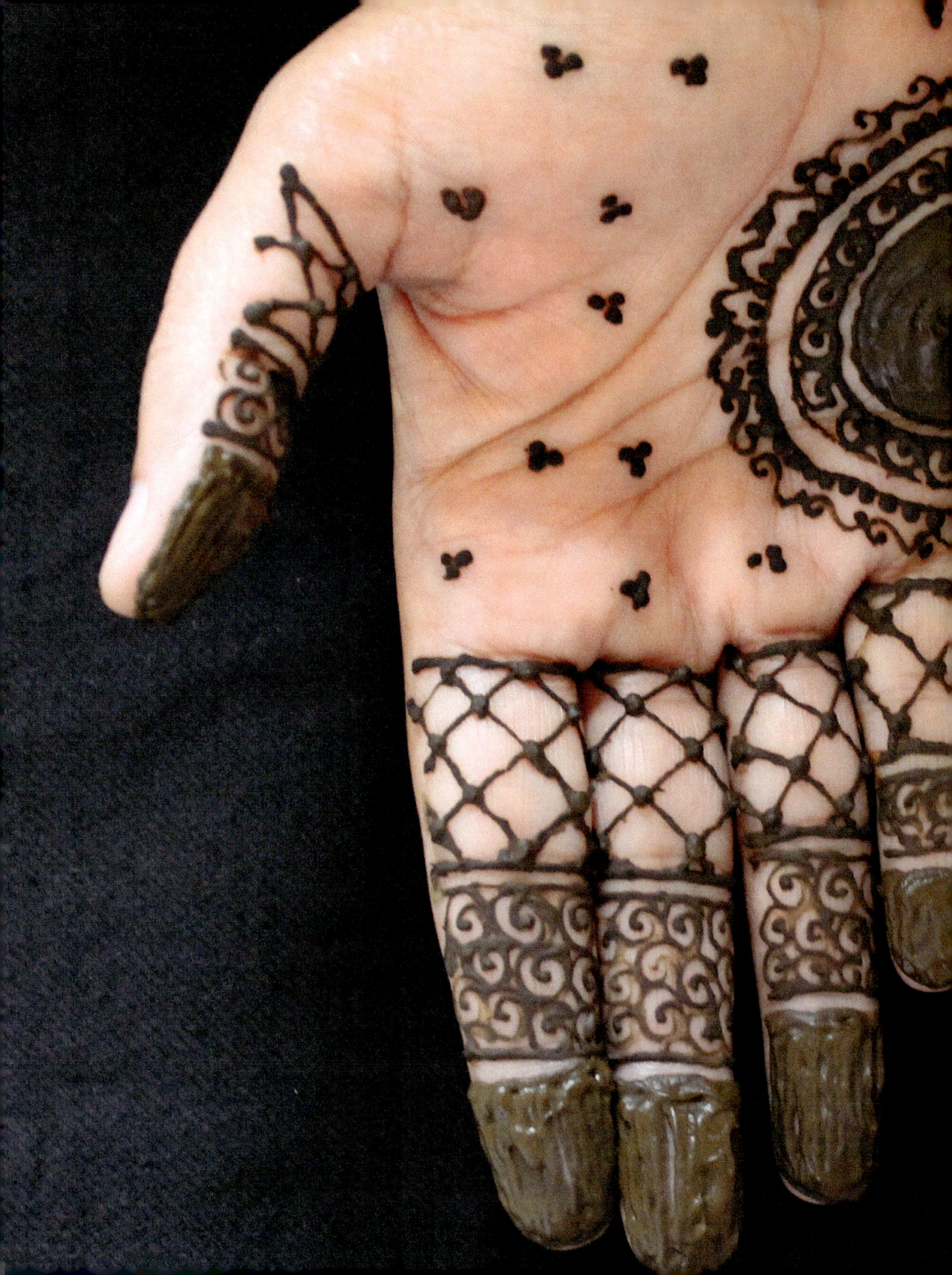

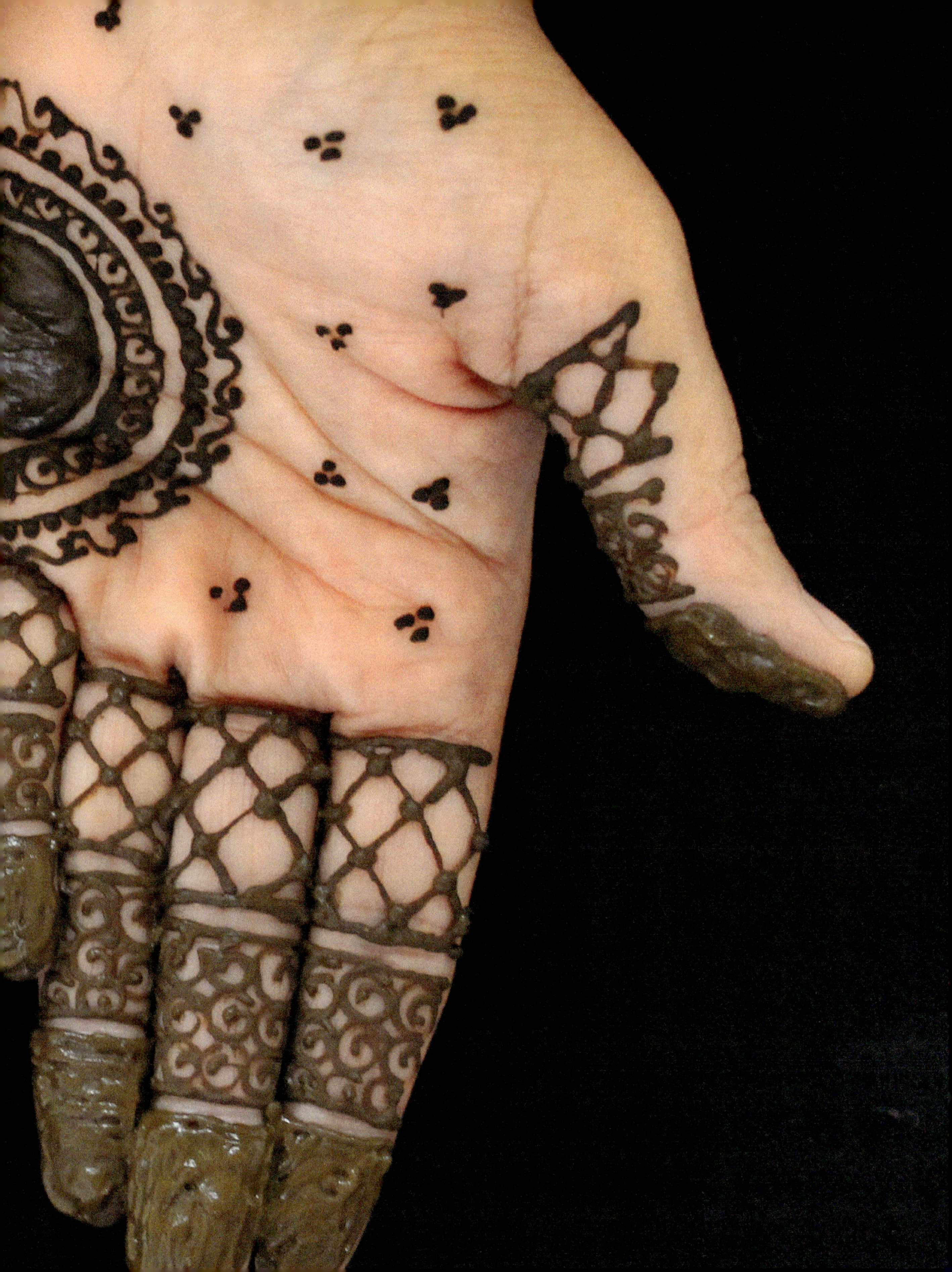

173

A trial run

The starting point would be a trial programme in local schools, to take place before making any future plans. I also recognised that I wouldn't get very far without having partners from within the South Asian communities. In this I was fortunate from the start. I asked my neighbour, Nusrat Rahman, if she knew of any artists within the local Asian community. At first she shook her head…then she hesitated and said that she had a niece, Habiba, who was artistic. I asked if I could meet Habiba and Nusrat gave me her phone number. Shortly after I met up with Habiba in the library; she was only 19 and had just left high school. Naturally I wasn't confident that she would have enough experience for this work. But in fact she was perfect; bright and confident. Habiba was also fortunate to have well connected and supportive parents, who encouraged and helped her, and in turn her confidence was a source of inspiration. She was a talented henna artist in her own right, and her *mehndi* designs became a feature of the visual style that emerged from *Different Moons*.

Suhail Khan of *Apna Creatives* in Manchester introduced me to Shamshad Khan. Shamshad is an experienced Manchester-based poet and trainer, and I asked her to work as Lead Artist on Different Moons. Shamshad agreed and with Habiba's help she ran a pilot project at St. James School in Haslingden. St. James has an intake of close to 90% South Asian heritage and Muslim children, yet remains a Church of England School. Running these classes went a long way towards helping us clarify both our process and our objectives. We submitted a report on the pilot project to the Heritage Lottery fund with a plan for an ambitious 30 month programme. In this we were helped by having made contact with Yasmine Choudry at the Islamic Supplementary School, based at Haslingden Community Link. Yasmine was enthusiastic about our ideas and keen to participate in the project.

At first I thought we would be working with a community – the 'South Asian (heritage) community', but from the beginning Shamshad insisted that I thought of communities, plural. The good sense of this soon became obvious. There were three main language groups and other groupings too, largely based on religious differences, though much of this was almost invisible to an outsider like myself. There was also the fact that men and women from this cultural background often lived relatively separate lives, in part due to the fact that the local mosques were for the men only.

Habiba was from a Pashtun background; Shamshad from a Pakistani. The third member of the team, Arry Nessa, came along later, initially as a volunteer, and she was from a local Bangladeshi family and a Bengali speaker. So, quite by chance, each of the main language groups within the communities was represented at the heart of the Different Moons team.

Previous pages: Mehndi work by Habiba Shenza,
Opposite above: Islamic Fountain at The Whitaker, by Phil Milston
Opposite lower: Story-telling paper-cut carpet by Maryam Golubeva

Above: Habiba Shenza with her mehndi piece at the Whitaker
Opposite page left: Habiba Shenza and Shamshad Khan interviewing

The first year of *Different Moons* culminated in a big exhibition at the Whitaker, the local museum and art gallery in Rawtenstall. The exhibition was partly about telling the story of the South Asian communities in Rossendale. We installed listening posts so visitors could hear extracts from the interviews we had recorded. There were also examples of some of the powerful poems written in Shamshad's workshops. I commissioned animators to make short films inspired by some of the stories we recorded.

The second part was my personal response to the religious lives of the Muslim community. It was centred around a working fountain built by Phil Milston, using traditional Islamic forms. This was accompanied by a soundtrack (by Chris Davies) which help create a meditative space. This room proved surprisingly popular, and it wasn't uncommon for visitors to sit in the room for long periods The exhibition was extended and was ultimately open for 8 weeks in total, during which time it had 5000 visitors

The second year saw the publication of a book of poems from the various classes that had been led by Shamshad, and readings at Haslingden Library. This was a powerful testament both to Shamshad's mentoring and her vision. Both years saw successful melas and bazaars, along with film shows, theatre pieces and music events at the Boo.

In the final year we published the interview texts, bound in leather, which were donated to each of the local libraries. There was now no longer a complete deficit of material relating to Rossendale's South Asian communities.

Apna

We soon realised that it was local South Asian women who most participated in, and benefitted from, the *Different Moons* programme. This may have been because they had fewer opportunities and, as noted, were excluded from the life of the mosques. Arry Nessa, whose commitment and contribution to the project had grown and grown, and I had the idea of opening a pop-up centre in Haslingden for a few months. The initial idea was to show some of the work that had been in the Whitaker, and see if there was any enthusiasm from the communities for further workshops and classes. The Lottery project budget had a small contingency fund that we used for this, and we rented a small shop premises in the centre of town and organised an exhibition plus a few trial classes and events.

Arry and I were delighted by the success of this venture, which we called *Apna* (meaning 'yours' or 'ours' in both Urdu and Bengali). When the project was due to close there were complaints from many of the women for whom we had provided a safe place of their own. Community Link, through Hameeda Khan-Davey, already offered classes for South Asia women but these had an entrance charge and, in any case, they were in constant danger of closure through budget cuts.

When *Different Moons* came to its end Arry and I decided to try to keep *Apna* open. We were successful in applying for a small Arts Council grant and to a local trust fund, which enabled us to keep it afloat for another year. At first most of the activities were arts or crafts based, but soon language, health, well-being, current affairs and history workshops were offered, along with occasional larger scale events. In 2017, when the second grant came to an end, we decided to move *Apna* to the Dave Pearson Studio (which I manage) in order to further cut our costs.

Apna was then funded by a three-year grant from the Tudor Trust. Most weekdays it offered some activities for South Asian women, and during this period *Apna* was engaged in a major textile project with The Whitworth Art Gallery in Manchester that culminated in a 6-month exhibition at the gallery. There was a programme of regular Islamic Art exhibitions, and the building of a positive relationship with Manchester Road Methodist Church, which became the venue for cooking and many other classes, as well as an art installation created by Maryam Golubeva (see page 170).

By the end of 2019 the Tudor Trust grant had finished; Covid-19 arrived, and Arry Nessa moved to Swindon to start a new life. In its 5 years *Apna* had clearly been important in creating new creative opportunities for women of South Asian heritage and there are now several community programmes initiated by the women who came together at *Apna*. In short the opportunities involving women from these communities in Rossendale and beyond have developed considerably since 2014. *Apna* clearly played an important part in this process.

The Moonwatcher

34. THE MOONWATCHER, 2018

I had always hoped that the *Different Moons* project would eventually lead to a touring show based on the stories of first South Asian immigrants to Rossendale. Finding and recording those stories was at the core of *Different Moons*, so creating a new theatre piece seemed to be the obvious way of bringing all the threads together. When *Different Moons* came to its end in 2017 we were determined that we should achieve this. Horse & Bamboo's new Executive Manager, Esther Ferry-Kennington, agreed. Because of the terms of our contract with the Arts Council, however, it was a struggle to find the finance. Thankfully Esther and the Board encouraged us in pursuing the proposal, as we all felt that it would be the most fitting way to complete five years of a unique creative project.

Eventually a limited tour was put together; it resulted in a show we called *The Moonwatcher*. It had a small associated outreach programme that was mainly based in Nelson. From the beginning it was going to be written and directed jointly with the Manchester-based poet Shamshad Khan, who had overseen much of the *Different Moons* programme.

Shamshad and I spent a lot of time together working out an effective structure for the show. This needed to balance her writing with my visual work. As a result it was an almost entirely new concept for a Horse & Bamboo production. What we came up with was a spoken narration that sometimes stood entirely on its own. It was also required to integrate with largely visual sections, films, and a sound track by Arun Ghosh. The narration thus moved in and out of, and meshed with, a parallel visual narrative. We eventually decided on one masked performer, and one unmasked, who took on the role of narrator. Both performers came together for puppetry and song sections. This basic structure worked well.

Working with Shamshad as co-director threw up memories for me of working with Sam Ukala in the late 1990s. Not surprisingly, some of the same issues arose too, as our practices and approaches were very different. Inevitably my experience was further removed from the source material than for Shamshad, whose life experience was that of a woman of South Asian background living and working in England.

A final tour

Early on it became apparent that it was going to be impossible to put together a suitably dramatic story using a limited cast if it was based solely on material gathered from our interviews. It's possible that we could have chosen to create a more documentary style of production. However neither of us wanted to take that route. Instead we agreed that Shamshad should introduce elements from her own life and experience into the story. We tried hard to keep aspects of the Rossendale interviews whenever possible. Nevertheless the introduction of Shamshad's own family stories had a profound impact on the direction of our show.

The Moonwatcher was my final work for Horse & Bamboo, both as co-writer and co-director. Fittingly, it was a completely new challenge. Not just in the way that any new theatre piece is, but in looking for a way to balance words, music and images. We ultimately did justice, and gave proper space, to Shamshad's powerful and emotionally rich language. At the same time we also created an integrated and arresting visual world. I felt that we finally managed both of these things successfully, although it was sometimes a struggle. The words and the images began trading off one another in fascinating ways, and never predictably. We were helped enormously by Arun's music, which for me could hardly have been better. He provided us with an emotional structure that supported the unfolding story perfectly. Equally powerful were Kain Leo's animated films, which took both the narrative and imagery further than I had imagined was possible. Again, they contributed a lot to the overall impact of the piece.

We were helped by finding two performers who really rose to the challenge. They were Gemma Khawaja, a puppeteer with *Norwich Puppet Theatre* who took on the masked roles brilliantly. Gemma lacked previous experience of mask-work, but responded with a puppeteer's insight. Hannah Kumari had the difficult role of speaking Shamshad's lines, which she did with real presence and authority. Hannah played the daughter and narrator, leading the audiences through the complex twists and turns of the story.

After 40 years my final taste of touring theatre was joining Gemma and Hannah for several days on the road in Scotland and North-East England, along with Leon Smith, the technician with the show. The venues included Universal Hall at Findhorn near Moray, an interesting and special place that the company had visited on a number of occasions during our horse-drawn days. Several people at Findhorn remembered those earlier visits, and reminisced with us about those old shows. People remembered the company camping in their gardens, and our grand clattering arrival with horses and wagons. In those last few days with *The Moonwatcher* team I re-experienced enough of the companionship, hard-work, good humour and the powerful commitment to a show and to its audience, to remind me just why taking stories out into the world in this way had sustained me – and our company, and all those artists, performers and audiences whose lives we had touched for such a long and unforgettable time.

From Royal Exchange Studio:

"Such a compelling story, so innovative with the puppet/human dynamic (that) brought something completely original to theatre."

"Fantastic music, visuals & most of all performance by brilliant actors. What an incredibly moving & powerful show."

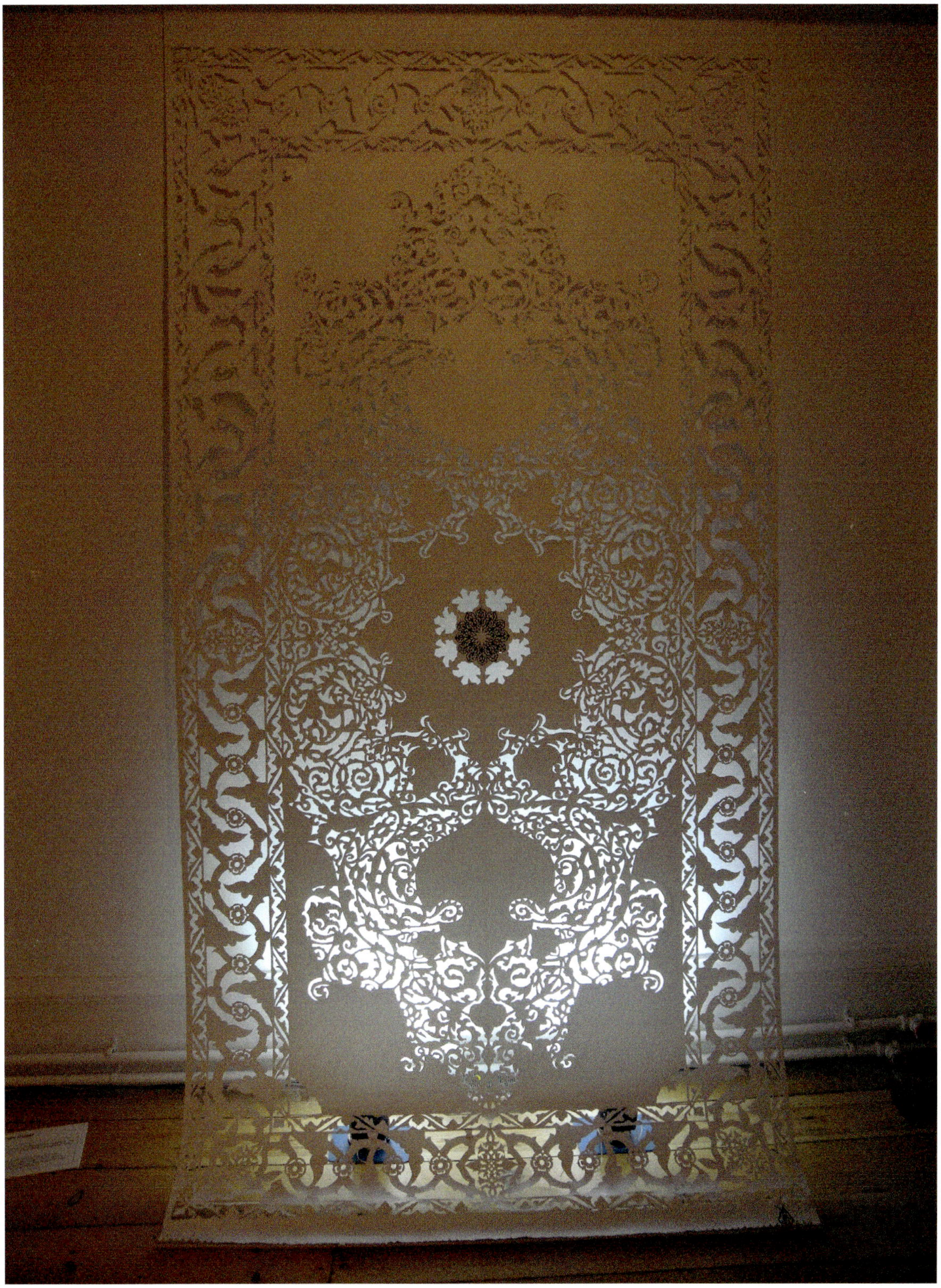

CODA

Throughout these years at Horse & Bamboo we also undertook many smaller projects. From touring the province of Sevilla in Andalucia immediately after the Franco years, through a Millennium kiln-firing on my small-holding, a history of the Lancashire Cricket League to shows especially designed for a primary school audience.

These were often memorable and highly enjoyable events. One that I remember particularly fondly was *The White Stag Cantata*, performed at our new Waterfoot base in 1998. It was poetic elegy for the Forest of Rossendale, in the shape of a celebration of the return of deer to the Valley after a long absence. Strongly visual of course, and with powerful choral and instrumental music directed by Loz Kaye. It also included spoken testimonies from local people:

*

"We were cutting wood and bundling it into the van. All of a sudden there was a commotion in the woods, the breaking of twigs, and a dog baying. Then a flurry of activity, which we couldn't see properly because of the density of trees, but then there was a white stag flashing through the glade into the thicker coverts. The noise was made by the dog, crashing around in pursuit. Our own dogs joined in immediately and disappeared into the woodland. All this happened in just a few seconds, and as quickly as it came upon us, everything returned to normal. Except we had lost our dogs. The owner of the first dog came by 'Oh, it happens all the time nowadays, they never catch them. Recently the deer have moved back into these woods from Bowland'. He carried on calling his dog. It took us 20 minutes of calling, too, before ours returned."

"It was late, well after midnight. It had been a good evening at the Station, and things went on later than usual for a Thursday night. Anyway, as I was walking past the Snig Hole path, the one which runs from the Bridge past the park, I heard a rustling. It was a still night, so obvious that something was up. I stopped dead, then carried on again. As I passed the Bridge pub, and started uphill the rustling started again and I looked around and saw it. Standing in the middle of the road, a full-grown stag with antlers. It was still, I'm not even sure it caused the rustling as it was so still. But when I moved towards it ever so slightly, it ran off – again really silently, and within a few seconds it disappeared. It was strange.... Stags haven't been seen around here for years."

Now people have built
Houses and tents in the forest
They inhabit the same, and when once before
There was nothing but deer
And other wild beasts
There is now by the people industry and labour

"We were pulling onto the A56. It's a dual carriageway, but with road works it was down to one lane. The other lane, behind the rows of cones, was being used as a store for cement slabs, kerbings and other items that were going to be used on the roadworks. Then, all of a sudden, I saw it. Sitting among the kerbings – a fully grown stag, graceful and elegant and in a resting position. As the car moved up to it I realised that it was dead, for it didn't move at all – and it was only a few yards from the stream of traffic. Yet it looked unharmed, and oddly peaceful. The traffic immediately took me away. It was disturbing seeing that beautiful creature there, in such an unfriendly situation. I couldn't shake the image – of the creature sitting among the roadworks – for ages."

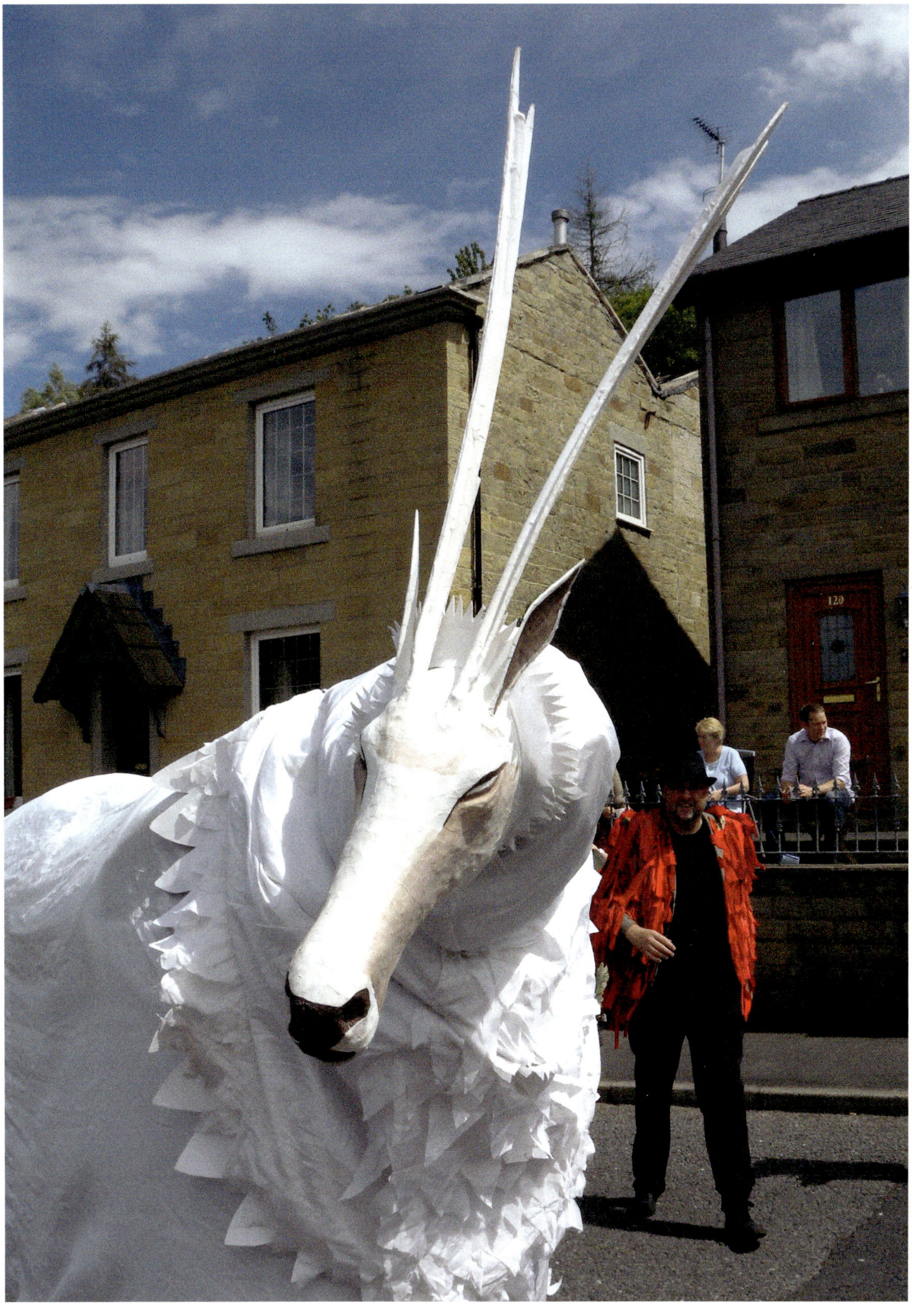
120

CAST LIST

1. The Ballad of Ellen Strange 1978
BOB FRITH, MAX BULLOCK (m), KEITH BRAY (m), GAIL KLEVAN (m), MAGGIE MARIGLIANI (m), GWYN JONES, SUE AUTY, DAVE CHADWICK, MALA SIKKA and students of Manchester School of Art Foundation Course.

2. Pictures From Brueghel 1979
BOB FRITH, FRANK BERBEE, MAGGIE MARIGLIANI, MALA SIKKA, KEITH BRAY (m), MAX BULLOCK (m), WIN HUNT (h), with SUE GOODWIN and BRAM GROOTHOF

3. The Home-made Circus 1980
BOB FRITH, RON PEPPERKAMP, FRANK BERBEE (m), WIN HUNT (h), ANNA NEAVE, LAURA BARNES, SAM RICHARDSON, DAVE CHADWICK, GWYNETH LAMB (m), PETER LINDHOUT, KAREN LANCEL, BRAM GROOTHOF (m), DAVE COOK (m).

4. Little Heads (Shouldn't Wear Big Hats) 1981
BOB FRITH, PAUL KERSHAW, SUE AUTY, EDWARD TAYLOR, ANDREW MILNE BERESFORD,
KEITH BRAY (m), PETER LINDHOUT, JAKE, FIONA FRANK, ADRIAAN KRABBENDAM, GILL PEARSON, WIN HUNT (h), KAY KENNEDY.

5. The Woodcarvers Story 1982
BOB FRITH, PAUL KERSHAW, JAY VENN (h), MALA SIKKA, AMANDA SPEED, BARBARA NICHOLLS,
MELISSA WYER, SUE GOODWIN, KEITH BRAY (m), DAVE GILES (m), KAY KENNEDY (maker), BRIAN KNOX (tech)

6. Needles In a Candleflame 1983
BOB FRITH, KEITH BRAY (m), DAVE GILES (m), MELISSA WYER, ADAM STRICKSON, MOIRA HIRST (h), RONA LEE, LUANA DEE, CLAIRE HEWLETT, AMANDA SPEED

7. Seol 1988
BOB FRITH, MICK WILSON (m), SALLY MARTIN (admin), MERIGAN MARTIN, MOIRA HIRST (h), ADAM STRICKSON, MELISSA WYER, ALAN KENNEDY (m), KATHY STRACHAN, BERNARD TINDALL.

8. Tales From a Maskshop 1986
BOB FRITH, MELISSA WYER, KAY KENNEDY, PAUL KERSHAW, MOIRA HIRST (h), ANNE BARBER, DAVE KING (m), STEPH BUNN, MARY PLUMB, SALLY MARTIN (admin).

9. An Roth/The Wheel 1987/8
BOB FRITH (wr/dir), TIM BENDER, TIM PETTER (m), DAVE KING (m), STEPH BUNN, JILL SWALES, ELE WOOD (h), ANNE BARBER, MARY PLUMB (m), KAY KENNEDY, THERESA WILDING, BRETT HORNBY (m), LIZ MATHER.
The Wheel: as above but also with the addition of SARAH FRANGLETON and MOIRA HIRST, without STEPH BUNN, JILL SWALES, KAY KENNEDY, THERESA WILDING.

10. The Plaited Path 1989
BOB FRITH (wr/dir), JO KING, CHRISTY EVANS, GARY HILL, SAM PAECHTER, JO POCOCK, ELE WOOD (h), SARAH FRANGLETON, JOHN MORETON (m and admin), KEITH BRAY (m), MINTY DONALD, NICK MILLAR, ANNE BARBER, JILL PENNY, BARRY LEE (h).

11. The Wheel 1990
Horse-drawn: BOB FRITH (wr/dir), DAVE KING (m), TIM PETTER (m), MARY PLUMB (m), MOIRA HIRST (h), SARAH FRANGLETON, JO KING, ANDREW PURVIN, MARK BROWN, TIM BENDER, ELE WOOD (h).
Motorised: GARY HILL, MAFALDA DA CAMARA, KEITH BRAY (m), BRAD HARLEY, JO KING, ANNE BARBER, SARAH FRANGLETON, DAVE KING (m).

12. The Flood 1991
BOB FRITH (wr/dir), JO KING, CHRISTY EVANS, GARY HILL, SAM PAECHTER, JO POCOCK, ELE WOOD (h), SARAH FRANGLETON, JOHN MORETON (m and admin), KEITH BRAY (m), MINTY DONALD, NICK MILLAR, ANNE BARBER, JILL PENNY, BARRY LEE (h).

13. A Strange (and Unexpected) Event! 1992/3/7
BOB FRITH (w/dir), BRAD HARLEY, STU BARKER (m), JO KING, ANNE BARBER, CLAIRE INGLEHEART (m), MARY KEITH, URSULA BURNS, FRANCES KING, NEVILLE CANN (m), MAFALDA DA CAMARA, GARY HILL, ELE WOOD (h), MOIRA HIRST (h), LOZ KAYE (m), NICKY FEARN, KATHY JONES, ANDREW KIM, KATHY BRADLEY, JILL PENNY, SARAH FRANGLETON, LIAM CARROLL (h), JOHN MORETON (admin), SALLY MARTIN (admin), MELANIE HORTON (marketing), PAUL BELL (childminder).

14. Dance of White Darkness 1994/5
BOB FRITH (wr/dir), LOZ KAYE (m), JILL PENNY, NICKY FEARN, BRIAN PORTER, URSULA BURNS, FRANCES KING, MARY KEITH (m), VICKY JASSEY (m), JO KING, CHRISSY RUCKLEY, ELAINE KINGSTON, NEVILLE CANN (m), GEZ HEBBURN (m), GARETH JENKINSON (LX), DULCIE BEST (set), TC HOWARD (choreography), ELE WOOD (h), LIAM CARROLL (h).

15. Visions of Hildegard 1994/5/6
BOB FRITH (wr/dir), SARAH FRANGLETON, CLAIRE INGLEHEART, MARTIN PEARSON, LOZ KAYE, JO KING, LIAM CARROLL (h), JILL PENNY, LISA HARRISON, SUE PALMER

16. The Legend of the Creaking Floorboard 1997/8
BOB FRITH (wr/dir), LOZ KAYE (m), CHRIS DAVIES (m), JO KING, JONNY QUICK, RUTH NAYLOR-JONES, VICTORIA LEE, SUE PALMER, LISA HARRISON, CAROLINE THOMPSON, GRAHAM FELL (h), SUE DAY (h)

17. Harvest of Ghosts 1999/2000
SAM UKALA and BOB FRITH (wr/dir), 'FUNMI ODEWALE, LOZ KAYE (m), YUSUPHA MBOOB, KATHY KIM, VICTORIA LEE, DANIEL POYSER, GLEN WILSON, NICKY FEARN.

18. The Girl Who Cut Flowers 2000
BOB FRITH/ALISON DUDDLE (dir), JENNY BRENT, NICKY FEARN, STEFF RYAN, CHRIS DAVIES (m), GLEN WILSON (h).

19. Company of Angels 2005/6
BOB FRITH/ALISON DUDDLE (dir), NICKY FEARN, JILL PENNY, KATHY KIM, ANDREW KIM, LOZ KAYE (m), JONNY QUICK, VICTORIA LEE

20. Little Leap Forward 2007-10
ALISON DUDDLE (dir), BOB FRITH (design), LOZ KAYE (m), JONNY QUICK, MARK WHITAKER, NICKY FEARN, KATHY KIM

21. Veil 2008
BOB FRITH (wr. dir), LOZ KAYE (m), NABIL MUSA, FRANCES MERRIMAN, ZOILO LOBERA, TRACY BARGATE, TESS HILLS, ERIK KNUDSEN (film), ALISON DUDDLE (making), KATHERINA RADEVA (set design and make)

22. Deep Time Cabaret 2011
BOB FRITH (wr. dir), JONNY QUICK, SONYA MOORHEAD, MARK WHITAKER, LOZ KAYE (m), STEFF LEE (film), TRACEY HOLLAND (film), ALISON DUDDLE (making).

23. Angus, Weaver of Grass 2012/13
BOB FRITH (wr. dir), JONNY QUICK, MARK WHITAKER, MAIRI MORRISON, LOZ KAYE (m), M.J. DEANS, FRANCES MERRIMAN, JORDANNA O'NEILL also JOANNE B KAAR, ALISON DUDDLE and VANESSA CARD (making), DANIELLA ORSINI and ELLIE CHANEY (animation), KIRSTY BLACKHALL (m)

24. The Moonwatcher 2018
SHAMSHAD KHAN (wr), BOB FRITH (dir), GEMMA KHAWAJA, HANNAH KUMARI, ARUN GHOSH (m), LEON SMITH (tech), KAIN LEO (film),

wr – writer
dir – director
m – musician
h – horses

ACKNOWLEDGEMENTS

First and foremost the obvious needs to be said – that without the enormous dedication, skill and artistry of the many, many talented people who, over 40 years, came together to create these shows, events and other productions at Horse & Bamboo, none of this would have been even remotely possible. To all of you I offer my sincere thanks and deepest gratitude for your unflagging commitment to all of this.

To Jill Penny, who encouraged me to continue with this book when I was full of doubts about it, and who then read and reread my various drafts, regularly coming back with wise suggestions and advice. Her support and genuine warmth towards the project has really helped to keep it going.

Also to David Chatton Barker, for his help in putting the words and images into a coherent design. David's own work continues to act as a constant inspiration, and in so many ways it takes me back half a century to those especially raw and exciting early years when everything seemed as if it was an experiment.

I've tried my best to credit all of the cast and others who directly supported these productions, but I acknowledge that I may well have overlooked some, and for this I can only ask forgiveness. I also recognise that the company has increasingly depended on a growing team of administrators and technicians who I've generally bypassed in this memoir of mine. So, to Sue Williams, Sally Martin, Liz Smith, Gill Pearson, Peter Cooke, John Moreton, Richard Hall, Ian Marsh, Andrew Rawlinson, Liz Mutch, Simon Ruding, George Harris, Christine Eddowes, Helen Jackson, Melanie Horton, Louise Milburn, Phil Milston, Helen Hughes, Elma Ikin, Esther Ferry-Kennington and – forgive me - many others besides, here's a small behind-the-scenes thank you and recognition of your vital contributions to the making of our theatre. Similarly, credit must be given to those people who since the early 1980s served on the Board of the company. Their input was often invaluable and many of the Chairs and Members became close friends.

Finally, to Kay for her consistent support, tolerance and love.

CREDITS

The majority of photographs in the book were taken by myself. The prints and graphics are also mine.

A few photographs were taken by others. There will be some too that I've collected but whose authorship I've forgotten, so profound apologies to anyone whose work is included here but has gone uncredited. Thanks also to Neville Cann for access to his archive.

Otherwise:
        Kirby 25 (upper)
        Alex Levac 30 (upper two), 31
        Rod Varley 23 (upper), 24. 26 (both)
        Dennis Thorpe (The Guardian) 59/60, 62 (both), 64 (lower left)
        Rod Young 87 (all), 107/8, 111, 112 (all)
        James Ravillious 79 (both), 81, 82 (all), 83 (all) 84 (top right and lower)
        Ian Tilton 146 (right), 147/8, 149, 150, 151, 152 (all), 153, 155 (all), 156, 157 (upper) , 158 (all)
        The Guardian 109

Horse + Bamboo